# SWEET MANDARIN
## COOKBOOK

# SWEET MANDARIN
# COOKBOOK

Classic and contemporary Chinese recipes with gluten- and dairy-free variations

## HELEN & LISA TSE

Photography by Gareth Morgans

Kyle Books

Published in 2014 by Kyle Books
www.kylebooks.com
general.enquiries@kylebooks.com

Distributed by National Book Network
4501 Forbes Blvd., Suite 200
Lanham, MD 20706
Phone: (800) 462-6420
Fax: (800) 338-4550
customercare@nbnbooks.com

ISBN: 978-1-909487-07-9

Library of Congress Control Number: 2013957926

Helen and Lisa Tse are hereby identified as the authors of
this work in accordance with Section 77 of the Copyright,
Designs and Patents Act 1988

Text © Helen and Lisa Tse 2014   Photographs © Gareth
Morgans 2014 except photo on page 2 (top left) © Helen
Tse 2014   Design © Kyle Books 2014

Editor: Vicky Orchard
Design: Jane Humphrey
Photography: Gareth Morgans
Food Styling: Sunil Vijayakar
Props Styling: Rachel Jukes
Production: Nic Jones and David Hearn

Color reproduction by ALTA London
Printed and bound in Singapore by Tien-Wah Press

*This book is dedicated to God, who makes all things possible; our beloved grandma Lily
Kwok, who is in Heaven, and to our sweet family: Mabel, Eric, Lisa, Helen, Janet, Jimmy, Peter,
Katherine, and Sam.*

God is indeed good. This cookbook has been cooking and simmering for over a
hundred years with recipes written down on the backs of envelopes and memorized
by heart as if they were nursery rhymes. My great-grandmother, grandmother, and
mother are the unsung heroes behind these recipes. We vow to continue the family
culinary journey through the Sweet Mandarin restaurant, cooking school, and range
of Sweet Mandarin sauces.

Thank you to Kyle Cathie and her very talented team, in particular Vicky Orchard,
who have embraced our family and our family recipes. Your unwavering support and
ability to help us spread the word about this book are amazing and we are so excited
to be on this unique journey with you. Thanks also to Gareth Morgans, Sunil Vijayakar,
and Rachel Jukes for the amazing photographs and food styling.

It was these recipes and the stories behind them that led to my first book, an
autobiography called *Sweet Mandarin*, which was published in 2007, but for a
few years, I held off publishing the recipes because of the loss of our beloved
grandmother Lily Kwok—the utter pain stopped me in my tracks and I put down my
pen until now. Time really does heal all wounds and I am so grateful to Kyle for giving
us a chance and publishing our family cookbook. This is not just any cookbook and
it is certainly more than a labor of love—it's a way of life that we live and breathe
every day. I'm inspired by Kyle Cathie's calm aura and determined attitude to
publishing our book worldwide and have absolute confidence that with Kyle, we
will finally be able to share our family recipes with you, wherever you may be in the
world. The Chinese proverb says "A Journey of a thousand miles starts with one step."
And I thank you for buying our book and joining our culinary journey.

Our heartfelt thanks also go to Anne Kibel, our agent and friend. From that
first phone call to meeting for a coffee in Hampstead, we knew that with your
enthusiasm, steer, and belief in us we will finally have a voice—to tell our story and
help others through our cooking. Sometimes you have more faith in us that we do
in ourselves, and that encouragement is truly humbling—we will do you proud
and we will make our mark in this world—in a sustainable and thoughtful way.

Finally, thank you to every single customer who we have cooked for and who has
bought our gluten-free sauces and in particular our Barbecue, Sweet Chile, and
Sweet and Sour sauces, this book is dedicated to you all. Without your business,
support, tweets, Facebook friends, Youtube likes and love, our family wouldn't be
here today to tell the tale and share these delicious recipes.

Scan the QR code opposite to watch our cooking videos online.
Tweet us @sweetmandarin or visit our Sweet Mandarin Sauces Facebook page.

# CONTENTS

# INTRODUCTION

"There are many things in the world that divide us—but one thing that unites us is food."—Helen Tse

These recipes originate from my grandmother, my mother, my twin sister Lisa, and me: three generations of independent Chinese women whose lives take place in Guangzhou in southern China in the 1920s, colonial Hong Kong in the 1930s, the Japanese invasion of Hong Kong, and a changing England from the 1950s to the present day. The times we have lived in have been unpredictable, but a love of food and a talent for cooking has pulled each generation through the most devastating upheaval.

My grandmother, Lily Kwok, was forced to work as an *amah* (servant) after the violent murder of her father. Crossing the ocean from Hong Kong in the 1950s, Lily went on to open one of Manchester, England's first Chinese restaurants—where her daughter Mabel, our mother, worked from the tender age of nine. But gambling and the Triads were pervasive in the Chinese immigrant community, and tragically my grandmother and mother lost the restaurant. It was up to my sisters and me to re-establish my grandmother's dream.

When we built our restaurant, Sweet Mandarin, we became the third generation of women restaurateurs and the fourth generation to make a living from our sauces. We are honored to share the family stories behind the recipes. Like Chinese cooking, our family fortunes contain layers of meaning and wisdom. Here is our family album, where food, anecdotes, and family folklore combine to be our heirloom. Food will always trigger memories and remind us of the kindness and cruelty of people and demonstrate how resilient humans can be. Sometimes it seems as if the most terrible times brought out the best recipes in my family.

I have written this book with my twin sister Lisa, and although I am the voice of this book, I speak for my sister and family. It is my desire that, through food, you get a snapshot into Chinese culture, history, and humor.

We are dedicated to making the dining experience inclusive to all and in particular to those who have allergies. We cater for the "free-from" markets with our gluten-free, dairy-free, nut-free range of Sweet Mandarin dipping sauces and our gluten-free menus at our Sweet Mandarin restaurant. To continue this, we've made suggestions for how to tailor the recipes if you follow a gluten-free or dairy-free diet.

This book lives and breathes our family's culinary tale and we hope that one day our paths may cross at Sweet Mandarin in Manchester, UK. We promise that you'll be enveloped by the sights and smells of a wonderful Chinese restaurant and enjoy totally unique dishes like Lily's curry and Mabel's clay pot chicken. It's a place we call home, and our passion is to share how easy and healthy Chinese food is.

All of our recipes have been tested at the Sweet Mandarin Cooking School, where we run courses, and some have also been tried out elsewhere—including on Gordon Ramsay's Aga, in the *Iron Chef* Kitchen Stadium, and even on a camp stove in rural China—so we are confident you will be able to recreate these dishes in your home kitchen.

We offer you this cookbook in the spirit of Lily's curry, Mabel's clay pot, and in honor of the exceptional women who gave us a chance in the world.

*Gambei*—Cheers!
Helen and Lisa

# TOP EIGHT TIPS

**Our top tips for basic Chinese cooking (eight is a lucky number in Chinese because it rhymes with the character "to get rich"):**

1  If you haven't got a wok yet, go out and buy one. It is one of the most versatile pieces of equipment and is one of the secret pieces of the jigsaw needed to make perfect stir-fries. Woks can also be used for steaming, deep-frying, and boiling. Their gently sloping concave shape ensures everything cooks evenly. When using a wok, always heat it fully over high heat before putting in the ingredients—this ensures that everything cooks quickly and vegetables stay crisp.

2  Most of the ingredients used in this book are widely available from mainstream supermarkets, but a few are available only from specialist Asian supermarkets.

3  Preparation is key to successful Chinese cooking. Make sure all the ingredients are washed and prepped before cooking. In many of the recipes, it is recommended that meat and vegetables are cut into similar sizes to ensure that they cook evenly.

4  The Chinese philosophy behind cooking involves balancing the yin and yang—for example, a yin ingredient such as ginger, which is hot, is balanced with a yang ingredient such as chicken, which is cooling. There are five key flavors in Chinese cuisine—sweet, sour, spicy, savory, and umami—at least one of these flavors is present in every recipe in the book.

5  For perfect, fuss-free rice, invest in a rice cooker. Chinese rice cookers are foolproof. I have recently come across a ceramic one, which cooks rice in 9 minutes in a microwave—now that's impressive!

6  Don't be afraid of garlic, ginger, or scallions, also known as the holy trinity in Chinese cooking. When cooked, these strong flavors mellow out and infuse the dish with a light perfume rather than intense grating flavors.

7  Don't scrimp on the sauce, as this is what will bring the dish alive. Many of the sauces can be made in advance and stored in the fridge until needed (see pages 14–15 for recipes). There are some really good sauces available from supermarkets if you don't have time to make your own.

8  Potato starch is used throughout the book for thickening sauces and binding ingredients together. It is gluten-free and flavorless. Where a recipe asks for potato starch mixture, combine 1 tablespoon of potato starch with 4 tablespoons of cold water and stir or whisk into a boiling sauce right at the end. Make sure you mix in the potato starch mixture thoroughly, stirring until the sauce thickens. If you don't have potato starch, you could always use cornstarch instead as this is also gluten-free.

# PANTRY

The list below is a few essentials that are handy to keep in the pantry because they are frequently used in a variety of dishes and are a great way to add flavor to recipes.

**Rice**—lasts for months in an airtight container and comes in numerous varieties e.g. long grain, basmati, jasmine, brown, red, or glutinous (which incidently does not have gluten).

**Noodles**—dried noodles last for months in an airtight container and come in thick or thin sizes.

**Soy sauce**—made from fermented soy beans— available in dark (for color) or light (for saltiness).

**Hoisin sauce**—a sweet sauce made from soy beans (not seafood) and perfect with Aromatic Crispy Duck (see page 58).

**Sweet chile sauce**—our own Sweet Mandarin version is gluten-free, with no monosodium glutamate (MSG), and is perfect for dipping or cooking with.

**Barbecue sauce**—our Sweet Mandarin variety is gluten-free, with no MSG and perfect for dipping or cooking with.

**Sweet Mandarin sweet and sour sauce**—gluten-free, no MSG, perfect for dipping or cooking with.

**Fermented black beans**—fermented in salt giving an intense flavor and used for dishes such as Chicken with Sweet Peppers and Black Beans (see page 68).

**Chile bean paste**—chiles, garlic, and soy beans fermented for over 40 days.

**Sesame oil** –made from sesame seeds, this has a wonderful, distinctive, aromatic smell that enhances any dish.

**Shaoxing wine**—a bit like sherry and used for dishes like the Salt and Chile Squid (see page 45).

**Five spice powder**—a mix of star anise, cloves, Chinese cinnamon, Szechuan pepper, and fennel seeds.

**Potato starch or cornstarch**—both gluten-free and used to make a light batter or mixed with water to thicken sauces.

**XO sauce**—made from dried scallops and chiles with an intense umami flavor—useful for enhancing fried rice dishes or meat dishes.

**Star anise**—a dried, star-shaped pod with an aniseed flavor.

# UTENSILS

**These are the basic utensils that make up a Chinese kitchen. The wok is the most important piece of equipment when cooking Chinese dishes. We have included other utensils here, which are non-essential but still useful.**

**Wok**—this is a round-bottomed cooking pan made of metal that is extremely versatile and can be used for stir-frying, steaming, pan-frying, deep-frying, poaching, boiling, braising, or making soup. There are all sorts of woks available—some are made of aluminum and are light, others are made of steel and are very heavy. Choose the wok that you feel most comfortable with in terms of weight. Aluminum woks are lighter and perfect for stir-frying. If you are planning to cook a lot of stews and braising dishes, the steel-bottomed woks are more robust. Woks generally don't come with a lid; these are sold separately, and if you are planning to cook a lot of steamed dishes, it would be worth investing in a lid for this.

**Cleaver**—a large knife with a rectangular blade, which is useful for chopping or crushing garlic or cutting through meat.

**Spider**—this resembles a sieve with a long handle and is useful for removing hot food from a liquid.

**Steamer**—usually made of bamboo and two layers high to allow the steam to travel up and cook the food contained within. This utensil is perfect for steaming fish or dumplings. Alternatively you can convert your wok into a steamer (see page 127).

**Chopsticks**—two sticks that are useful to pick up pieces of food. Wooden chopsticks without any colored patterns on them are useful utensils to test whether oil is hot enough for deep-frying. Dip the chopstick in the oil. If bubbles form around the stick, then the oil is hot enough to deep-fry.

# CUTTING MEAT

To ensure the ingredients cook evenly, it is important that everything is diced to the same size. For cutting meat, we use a Chinese cleaver.

# CHICKEN STOCK
## 清雞湯

- Gluten free
- Dairy free
- Egg free

*Makes 2 quarts*
*Preparation time 5 minutes*
*Cooking time 1 hour*

**8 chicken wings, weighing**
   **approx. 1¾ lbs.**
**1 large onion, roughly chopped**
**2-inch piece of fresh ginger, whole**
**3 quarts (12 cups) water**

**\*Lisa's tips**
*To make seafood stock, replace the chicken*
*wings with shrimp, preferably in their shells.*

Chicken stock is one of the key ingredients in Chinese cooking and is used as a base for many of the dishes in this book. This really simple Chinese recipe is for a light, delicious, and naturally sweetened stock.

Our grandmother, Lily Kwok, believes chicken stock has healing powers almost as powerful as the holy waters. Lily met our grandfather, Chan, under the most remarkable circumstances and this is what she fed him to nurse him back to health. The story goes like this... Lily was working as a maid and cook for an English family in Hong Kong when she saw the lifeless body of a young boy (who eventually became our grandfather) washed up on the docks. She raised the alarm to the English family, who took him to the hospital where he was resuscitated. When Chan opened his eyes, he saw Lily looking down at him, and, thinking she was an angel, he believed he had died. For days after this incident, Lily painstakingly restored the health of Chan with this chicken stock and she has sworn by the recipe ever since.

METHOD

Wash the chicken wings thoroughly. Put all the ingredients in a large saucepan, bring to a boil, and boil for 15 minutes.

Reduce the heat to low, cover the pan with a lid, and simmer for 45 minutes, during which time the liquid will reduce down to approx. 2 quarts. Skim off any scum from the surface with a slotted spoon and strain the stock through a sieve into a clean pan—the boiled chicken wings will be extra tender and can be eaten. Either use the stock straight away or pour it into ice-cube trays and store in the freezer until needed.

# VEGETABLE STOCK
# 蔬菜湯

*Gluten free*

*Dairy free*

*Egg free*

*Makes 2 quarts*

*Preparation time 5 minutes*

*Cooking time 45 minutes*

**3 large carrots, peeled and cut into
1-inch pieces**

**2 large onions, diced**

**2 leeks, cut in half and washed
thoroughly**

**2-inch piece of fresh ginger, whole**

**3 quarts (12 cups) water**

**\*Lisa's tips**

*This is perfect as a base for vegetable soup.
Add peas, beans, and any other vegetables,
that you have in your fridge or pantry.*

I learned this recipe for vegetable stock from a Filipina woman named Carol working in Hong Kong, whom I discovered quite by accident one Sunday morning in 2002 outside the HSBC tower, a giant Norman Foster–designed skyscraper that stares out across Victoria Harbour. As I approached the tower, I was startled to hear a loud, high-pitched clucking noise that sounded like a flock of flamingos. Intrigued, I walked toward the noise and saw a group of Filipina women cooking over a camp stove. I asked my mother who they were, and she explained that they were *amahs*, or maids, who gathered at this makeshift meeting place every Sunday to cook and chat because they had nowhere else to go on their day off. As I moved closer to the crowd, I saw a woman stirring a bubbling pot of vegetables, and she waved me over to try. She poured me a small plastic cup of the hot liquid and I carefully drank it. It was so sweet, delicious, and light that I wanted to learn her recipe. Communicating mainly by pointing, nodding, and smiling, she explained that the vegetables were seconds or "no good," because they were slightly bruised or dried at the ends. Her employer had given her the vegetables to throw away, but Carol believed there was still plenty of life left in them so she brought them along to cook. This is her recipe; it is a perfect, forgiving way to use any vegetables that are just about to pass their best-before date.

METHOD

Put all the ingredients in a large saucepan, bring to a boil, and boil for 15 minutes.

Reduce the heat to low, cover the pan with a lid, and simmer for 30 minutes, during which time the stock will reduce to approx. 2 quarts. Strain into a clean pan and use immediately or pour into ice-cube trays and store in the freezer until needed.

# SWEET AND SOUR SAUCE

## 糖醋汁

This sauce can be used either as a dipping sauce, marinade or as a sauce to serve alongside individual recipes.

 *Gluten free*

*Dairy free*

*Egg free*

*Makes 1¼ cups*

*Preparation time 10 minutes*

*Cooking time 10 minutes*

**2 tablespoons ketchup**

**1 cup cold water**

**½ cup sugar**

**⅓ cup white wine vinegar**

**3 slices of lemon**

**3 slices of fresh ginger**

**1 tablespoon potato starch**

METHOD
Combine all the ingredients except for the potato starch in a small saucepan and bring to a boil over high heat. Add the potato starch and stir vigorously to thicken the sauce. Remove the pan from the heat and set aside to cool.

Store in a sealed container in the fridge and use within 2 weeks.

# SWEET CHILE SAUCE

## 甜辣醬

An exciting concoction of fresh red chiles mixed with garlic and vinegar that tickles the tongue. Perfect for livening up stir-fries, noodles, or salads or on the side as a zingy dip.

*Gluten free*

*Dairy free*

*Egg free*

*Makes 1¼ cups*

*Preparation time 15 minutes*

*Cooking time 10 minutes*

**4 long red chiles, finely chopped**

**3 garlic cloves, peeled**

**¼ cup white wine vinegar**

**½ cup sugar**

**1 cup cold water**

**1 tablespoon salt**

**1 tablespoon potato starch**

METHOD
Blend all the ingredients except for the potato starch in a blender. Pour the mixture into a small saucepan and bring to a boil over high heat. Add the potato starch and stir vigorously to thicken the sauce. Remove the pan from the heat and set aside to cool.

Store in a sealed container in the fridge and use within 2 weeks.

# BARBECUE SAUCE
# 烤肉調味汁

*Gluten free*

*Dairy free*

*Egg free*

*Makes 2 cups*

*Preparation time 10 minutes*

*Cooking time 10 minutes*

1¼ cups ketchup

1 cup cold water

½ cup red wine vinegar

1⅓ cups brown sugar

1 teaspoon Worcestershire sauce

2½ teaspoons mustard powder

2 teaspoons paprika

1 teaspoon salt

1 teaspoon freshly ground
   black pepper

A thick, fruity sauce that evokes memories of heady evenings. Perfect as a dip with shrimp crackers and other snacks, or as a marinade for meats.

METHOD

Combine all the ingredients in a small saucepan and whisk well until the spices have distributed evenly and the sugar has dissolved. Bring to a boil then remove the pan from the heat and set aside to cool.

Store in a sealed container in the fridge and use within 2 weeks.

Our mother believes that soups are the key to staying healthy. Although they were born into Cantonese families in Hong Kong and moved to the United Kingdom at a young age, our parents made sure that the tradition of soups was one distinct aspect of Chinese food culture that they instilled in us. A bowl of nourishing Chinese soup conjures up the same comfort as, and even nostalgia for, childhood times eating the family's homemade soups. There is a rich tradition behind the preparation of soup, and cooking it is a culinary art that has been perfected over thousands of years. It is a deep-rooted and much-loved dish in Chinese cuisine, so much so that if you get invited to a friend's home for soup, then you know that you have been accepted into their family.

Chinese appetizers are also known as "dim sum," which means "touch the heart" when literally translated. Originally a Cantonese custom, dim sum is part and parcel of the Chinese tradition of *yum cha* or tea drinking. This harkens back thousands of years to the Silk Road, where weary travellers visited teahouses to enjoy dim sum appetizers, hot tea, and animated banter with other visitors. There are literally thousands of appetizers to choose from so we have provided a selection of our favorites.

湯和起動器

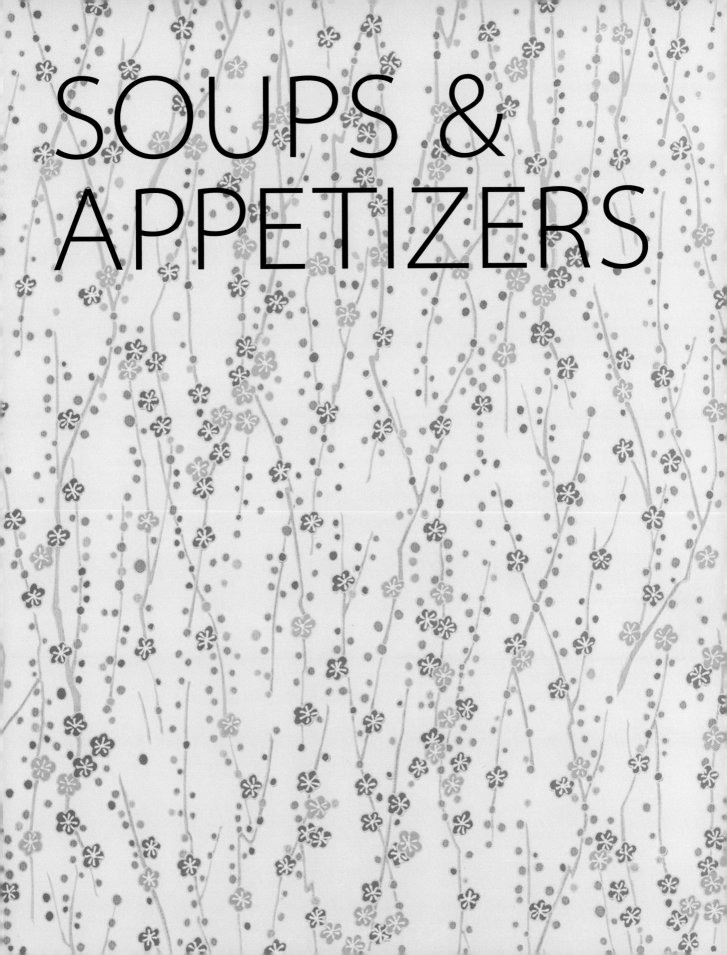

# SOUPS & APPETIZERS

# HOT AND SOUR SOUP
## 酸辣湯

*Replace the chile bean sauce with mashed fresh chiles. The sweet and sour sauce is gluten free.*

*Dairy free*

*Omit the egg*

*Serves 2*

*Preparation time 10 minutes*

*Cooking time 15 minutes*

**2½ cups chicken stock** *(see page 12)*

**¾ cup cooked diced meat, such as pork, chicken, ham, or *char siu*** *(see page 89)*

**¾ cup small, cooked, peeled shrimp**

**⅓ cup bamboo shoots**

**½ cup carrot strips**

**2oz tofu, cut into strips**

**1 teaspoon chile bean sauce**

**1 tablespoon white wine vinegar**

**½ cup sweet and sour sauce** *(see page 14)*

**½ teaspoon salt**

**¾ teaspoon sugar**

**2 tablespoons potato starch mixture** *(see page 8)*

**1 small egg, beaten**

**1 drop of sesame oil**

**\*Lisa's tips**

*This soup works equally well as a vegetarian alternative. Replace the chicken stock with vegetable stock (see page 13), omit the meat and shrimp, and replace with double the quantity of carrots and bamboo shoots.*

The first item on the menu at Sweet Mandarin when we opened our doors back in 2004 was Hot and Sour Soup, and this is what caught the attention of John, now one of our regulars, who walked through the door on day one to order this dish. John is now a dear friend and we owe him a huge vote of thanks for all his support in helping us get our gluten-free sauces off the ground and into supermarkets. Recently, we reminisced about that rainy day in November 2004 and he said that our friendship was cemented when I served him this soup. "It's the ultimate test of a good Chinese restaurant. Your Hot and Sour Soup was so good I had to get to know you, chef!" This is also a firm favorite with our sister Janet, who loves, loves, loves my Hot and Sour Soup! It certainly warms you up; the spicy sauces are wonderfully aromatic and enhance the flavor. Once you've perfected the balance of spicy and sour, you can sip away to your heart's content.

METHOD

Pour the stock into a wok or saucepan and bring to a boil. Add the cooked meat, shrimp, vegetables, and tofu and simmer for 3–4 minutes, stirring often. Mix in a generous teaspoon of chile bean sauce, and pour in the vinegar and sweet and sour sauce. Season with salt and sugar, stir well, and cook for about 5 minutes until boiling.

Once the soup is boiling, add the potato starch mixture and mix in vigorously—if you don't stir the soup, it will become gloopy in the center and watery around the edges.

Remove the wok from the heat and slowly swirl in 2 tablespoons of the beaten egg. Use a fork or the stirrer to mix the egg into strands to create an egg-drop effect, which is essentially thin swirls of egg. Return the wok to the heat for another 30 seconds to cook the egg. Add in a little drop of sesame oil and enjoy!

# CANTONESE WONTON DUMPLING SOUP
## 雲吞湯

Option 1: Omit the wonton wrappers.
Option 2: Use gluten-free flour rather than
all-purpose flour. Replace the dark soy
sauce with tamari or omit altogether.

Dairy free

Omit the egg

Serves 2

Preparation time 20 minutes

Cooking time 15 minutes

*For the wonton pastry*

**1²⁄₃ cups all-purpose flour, plus
   extra for dusting**

**5 eggs (1 whole egg and 4 egg yolks)**

**2 tablespoons water**

**1 teaspoon salt**

*For the filling*

**¼ lb ground pork**

**¼ lb raw, peeled large shrimp,
   deveined and coarsely chopped
   into small pieces**

**1 teaspoon salt**

**1 teaspoon sugar**

**1 teaspoon sesame oil**

**1 tablespoon potato starch**

**2 tablespoons water**

*For the soup*

**2½ cups chicken stock** *(see page 12)*

**¾ cup Napa cabbage, chopped into
   bite-sized pieces**

**1 teaspoon salt**

**1 teaspoon sugar**

**¼ teaspoon white pepper**

**1 drop of dark soy sauce**

**1 drop of sesame oil**

**1 teaspoon finely sliced scallions**

Literally translated, wonton means "swallowing a cloud." Every province in China boasts its own version of wontons, all of them with different fillings—from shrimp or pork to cabbage or bok choy—and its own trademark pleating technique.

Throughout China, food is used to heal the body and this is THE ultimate get-well-soon soup, especially if you have a sore throat. Why? Well, the dumplings are boiled so they are easy to swallow, and the clear broth warms the organs and comforts the soul. Try it next time you don't feel well.

METHOD

To make the wonton dough, put all the ingredients into a food processor and process to a firm dough. Turn out onto a lightly floured work surface and roll out as thinly as possible. Using a glass or cup (approx. 2 inches in diameter), cut out roughly 14 circles and dust lightly with flour. Cover with a damp cloth or plastic wrap until ready to use.

To make the filling, combine the ground pork and shrimp in a bowl and season with salt, sugar, and sesame oil. Add the potato starch and water and mix thoroughly with your hands to form a sticky paste. (Don't be tempted to use a food processor for this because you want to retain some texture.)

To assemble the wontons, put 1 teaspoon of the filling in the center of each wonton skin. Using your index finger, dampen one corner of the dough and fold over to form a half-moon shape. Crimp the edges by squeezing them together with your index finger and thumb to form a wavy pattern.

To cook the wontons, bring a pan of water to a boil, drop in the wontons, and simmer gently for 5 minutes. Drain thoroughly and set aside to rest in a soup bowl.

To make the soup, bring the chicken stock to a boil, add the Napa cabbage, salt, sugar, white pepper, soy sauce, and sesame oil, and simmer for 5 minutes. Sprinkle with the scallions.

To serve, pour the soup over the wontons and slurp away, filling your tummy with goodness.

# CHICKEN AND CORN SOUP
## 粟米雞湯

🌀 *Gluten free*

💚 *Dairy free*

🔵 *Omit the egg*

*Serves 2*

*Preparation time 5 minutes*

*Cooking time 10 minutes*

**2½ cups chicken stock** *(see page 12)*

**¾ cup diced cooked chicken breast**

**4 tablespoons corn**

**½ teaspoon salt**

**½ teaspoon sugar**

**2 tablespoons potato starch mixture**

   *(see page 8)*

**1 egg, beaten**

**1 drop of sesame oil**

**\*Lisa's tips**

*Very easy to make, but prepare everything in advance to make it even easier.*

Our parents were married in Bury in 1975 in a small traditional ceremony followed by a wedding banquet of huge proportions. My mother said that practically all the Chinese who were in Britain were invited—much to the horror of Dad, who had to foot the bill!

The first course was Chicken and Corn Soup. However, it turned out the guests couldn't eat it because the chef had been too enthusiastic with the salt—apparently he had never cooked for so many people in his life and ended up using a ladleful instead of a tablespoonful! Nonetheless, it didn't stop the celebrations, and our father vowed to make this soup for his wife when they went home—so that they would start things off on the right foot. To this day, they still talk about that salty soup and often remind me to watch the salt when teaching this dish at the Sweet Mandarin Cooking School. It's a delicious soup, but Dad is 100 percent correct—too much salt can ruin it.

We are often asked whether we make the soup in one big batch for our customers or whether it is made up to order. Well, the answer is that every bowl is freshly cooked to order as this retains the best flavor and, more importantly, it helps the soup hold together and stops it from being watery, which often happens with the big batch process. The secret to a great Chicken and Corn Soup is to use homemade chicken stock.

METHOD

Heat a wok on high heat and pour in the chicken stock. Add the cooked chicken and corn and season with salt and sugar. Bring the soup to a boil, add the potato starch mixture and mix vigorously for 1 minute until thick.

Remove the wok from the heat and swirl in 2 tablespoons of beaten egg, using a ladle to mix in a clockwise direction (see page 18). Return the pan to the heat for another 30 seconds to cook the egg. Finish with a drop of sesame oil and stir into the soup. Enjoy slurping from Chinese soup spoons.

# MY MOTHER'S CHICKEN'S FEET SOUP
## 雞腳湯

*Gluten free*

*Dairy free*

*Egg free*

*Serves 2*

*Preparation time 10 minutes*

*Cooking time 1 hour*

**3 tablespoons raw, unsalted peanuts**

**6 dried red dates**

**5 dried shiitake mushrooms**

**10–12 chicken's feet (these usually come prepacked, but at some Chinese or Asian stores you can select how many you want)**

**2½ cups water**

**1 tablespoon salt**

**\*Lisa's tips**

*Chicken's feet might make you scrunch your nose up in disgust, but really they are no more adventurous than oxtail or pig's trotters, which have become very popular in Michelin-starred restaurants.*

When our mother was pregnant with us, her knees were pained by the weight of the bump so Lily made her this soup to boost her cartilage. There was a surprise in the pregnancy—only Lisa had shown up in the last prenatal scan but, in fact, I was hidden behind her and not even the doctors guessed Mom was having twins. No wonder the bump was so heavy!

If you are feeling adventurous and want to delve into the heart of authentic China, then this recipe is for you. It's our mother's favorite soup because it helps her joints and eases her arthritis. The added benefits are that this soup is full of calcium and collagen—perfect for maintaining the firmness and moisture in her beautiful skin. This silky soup is not for the faint-hearted; however, if you can get past the toenails of the chickens, it is delicious.

METHOD

Soak the peanuts, red dates, and mushrooms in hot water for 15 minutes; drain. Keep these ingredients whole.

Clean the chicken's feet by removing the outer layer of skin and trimming the claws (if not already done by your supermarket).

Pour the water into a medium saucepan and bring to a boil. Add the chicken's feet, peanuts, dates and mushrooms, reduce the heat to its lowest setting, and simmer for 1 hour. Season to taste with salt.

# WINTER MELON AND WOLFBERRY SOUP
## 冬瓜枸杞湯

● Gluten free
♥ Dairy free
○ Egg free
Serves 4
Preparation time 15 minutes
Cooking time 1¼ hours

**10 cups water**

**14oz pork spare ribs**

**10oz winter melon, peeled and cut into 2-inch dice**

**1 tablespoon dried shrimp, soaked in lukewarm water for 10 minutes (optional)**

**1 teaspoon white peppercorns, lightly pounded**

**1 dried honey date**

**⅓ cup wolfberries or goji berries**

**salt, to taste (optional)**

### *Lisa's tips

*If you can't get winter melon, use 2½ cups diced zucchini instead. If you can't find honey dates, you can use ordinary dates.*

When we go for dim sum (also known as *yum cha*, which literally translates as "drink tea"), we bump into lots of family friends, and one of those is Mr. Dong. He grows his own winter melon, as does our dad. The only problem is that Mr. Dong always boasts about how big and majestic his winter melons are, which irks our dad. One summer, back in 1988, Dad decided to try to grow the biggest winter melon. He didn't succeed, but he did end up growing more than 60 of them in the backyard, which exasperated our mother who had to step over them to hang the laundry out to dry. For weeks on end, she created recipes using the winter melon—and this is one of them. Whenever we make this amazing soup, it takes me back to the summer of 1988, to our childhood filled with laughter and food.

Winter melons (冬瓜 *dong gua*) can grow as big as a 20lb watermelon and look similar with their dark green skin, but their flesh is more akin to the neutral flavor of zucchini (which you could always use instead). Cooling winter melon is reputedly an excellent detoxifier and helps with weight loss. Although it is called the winter melon, it is actually a summer fruit.

## METHOD

Pour 4 cups of water into a large saucepan and bring to a boil. Add the ribs and boil for 10 minutes; this will cook off the scum. Drain through a colander, discarding the cooking liquid, and return the ribs to the pan.

Add the winter melon, reconstituted shrimp (if using), peppercorns, honey date, and wolfberries, cover with 6 cups of water, and bring to a boil. Boil rapidly for 15 minutes.

Reduce the heat to its lowest setting and simmer for another 45 minutes, by which time the soup should be sweet and full of flavor. Season with salt to taste.

# MISO SOUP WITH TOFU
# 味噌湯

♡ *Dairy free*

○ *Egg free*

*Serves 2*

*Preparation time 5 minutes*

*Cooking time 10 minutes*

3⅓ **cups dashi stock**

4 **tablespoons white or red miso paste**

3oz **silken tofu, cut into ½-inch cubes**

2 **tablespoons dried wakame seaweed**

⅓ **cup finely sliced scallions**

*For the Dashi stock*

1 **piece (approx. 7oz) of dried dashi or kelp (kombu), washed thoroughly**

1oz **dried bonito flakes (katsuobushi)**

2 **dried shiitake mushrooms, soaked in boiling water for 15 minutes or until reconstituted**

4 **cups water**

**\*Lisa's tips**

*Ensure the dashi stock is not boiling when you add the miso paste.*

*The ingredients for this stock won't be readily available from mainstream supermarkets, but you should be able to buy them online or from good Asian supermarkets (where ready-made dashi stock should also be available if you don't want to go to the trouble of making it yourself).*

Our grandmother lived through World War II, which saw Hong Kong endure years of Japanese occupation. At that point in her life, she was working as a maid to a Dutch chocolate maker located in Hong Kong who had won a contract to supply chocolate to the Japanese soldiers. She and her employer family learned Japanese and set sail for Japan, where Lily cooked side by side with Japanese cooks, swapping recipes, including this miso soup.

Today in Hong Kong, the Japanese influences are apparent for all to see. Miso soup is synonymous with Japanese sushi and is a favorite for many in Hong Kong and all over the world. This soup tastes totally different from Chinese soups because the dashi stock is flavored with dried fish, making it aromatic and full of umami flavor. Miso (みそ or 味噌) is a traditional Japanese seasoning, produced by fermenting rice, barley, and/or soybeans with salt and the fungus (kōjikin 麹菌). The result is a thick paste used for sauces and spreads and for mixing with dashi stock to serve as miso soup, a Japanese culinary staple.

METHOD

Pour the dashi stock into a saucepan and bring to a boil. Reduce the heat to a simmer while you prepare the miso paste.

Put the miso paste in a bowl and add 2–3 tablespoons of the hot stock. Stir to dissolve. Pour the mixture back into the pan of simmering soup.

Add the tofu and wakame seaweed and increase the heat to simmer gently for 5 minutes; do not allow the miso soup to boil or it will taste bitter.

Sprinkle with the finely sliced scallion just before serving.

DASHI STOCK

We call this lesser-known stock "sea stock" because it is made with kelp and bonito (fish) flakes. It is perfect to use in the recipe for miso soup.

Put the kelp, dried bonito flakes, and reconstituted shiitake mushrooms into a saucepan and cover with the water. Bring to a boil and boil for 10 minutes.

Reduce the heat to low and simmer for another 20 minutes. Use immediately or pour into ice-cube trays and freeze until needed.

# TUESDAY'S PORK RIB BROTH
## 排骨湯

◐ *Gluten free*

♥ *Dairy free*

◐ *Egg free*

*Serves 2*

*Preparation time 5 minutes*

*Cooking time 2 hours*

**14 cups water**

**1 lb pork spare ribs**

**2 carrots, peeled but left whole**

**2 radishes, washed but left whole**

**2-inch piece of fresh ginger, whole, smashed lightly with a rolling pin**

**2 teaspoons salt**

**½ cup fresh cilantro, roughly chopped**

**\*Lisa's tips**

*Any leftover broth could be used to flavor sauces and gravies. To make homemade stock cubes, simply pour the broth into ice-cube trays and freeze until needed.*

My twin sister Lisa, younger sister Janet, younger brother Jimmy, and I grew up in the family food business and lived above the shop. Like our parents and their parents, it was a way of life and we simply didn't know any different. All I knew was that we lived over the shop, ate from the shop, and worked in the shop. There was nothing else. Days of the week were marked by what was cooking in the pot. As a child I always remember Tuesday being soup day. Our mother would fill a big, silver saucepan (industrial sized) with over 50 spare ribs to make the ultimate stock, which was rich with flavor. After slow-cooking for two hours, to break down the protein and calcium in the bones, the spare-rib meat would be melt-in-the-mouth tender. Here I've tailored her recipe to serve two.

METHOD

Prior to making the soup, it is a good idea to blanch the ribs to reduce the amount of scum formed in the soup. Fill a large saucepan with 4 cups of water and bring to a boil. Add the ribs and simmer gently for 10 minutes. Drain, discarding the cooking liquid, and return the ribs to the pan.

Add the carrots, radishes, and ginger, and cover with 2.5 quarts of water. Bring to a boil and boil for 10 minutes. Reduce the heat to the lowest setting and simmer for another 1½ hours, by which time the rib meat should be falling off the bones and the broth will be deliciously sweet.

Season with salt and sprinkle with some chopped cilantro.

# HEALTHY FISH SOUP
## 魚湯

*Gluten free*

*Dairy free*

*Egg free*

*Serves 2*

*Preparation time 15 minutes*

*Cooking time 30 minutes*

**1 whole sea bream (or any white fish of your choice), weighing approx. 12oz**

**1 teaspoon salt**

**2 carrots, peeled and sliced into thick rounds**

**6 cups water**

**7oz spinach, washed (preferably with stems removed)**

**\*Lisa's tips**

*Ask your fishmonger to gut, gill, and scale your fish for you. If you are squeamish about fish bones, use monkfish; it only has one big bone, and the flesh is meaty like lobster.*

Our great-grandmother and great-grandfather were betrothed at the age of four and had an arranged marriage ten years later. Great-grandmother was dressed in red—for luck and good fortune—before being taken to the groom's home for the ceremony. From that day on, she never went back; she belonged to the Leung family by both civil and religious law and her duty was to obey and serve her mother-in-law. According to a poem by Wang Jian (王建), one of the ways a new bride could gain acceptance into her new family was to make soup, and fish soup showed a particular flair for cooking. Our great-grandmother swore by this soup because she believed the smooth, velvety texture calmed her mother-in-law's temper, which was incredibly short, and extinguished the fire in her eyes.

Soup is an important part of the Chinese diet, since many people believe it is unhealthy to drink cold drinks with a meal. You can use any white fish for this soup. I like to use sea bream, which is one of my favorite fish, because it is full of nutrients, creamy in texture, and opaque white in color.

METHOD

Clean the bream thoroughly and sprinkle the salt over its body and in the cavity.

Put the whole fish and carrots into a saucepan, pour in the water, and bring to a boil. Boil for 5 minutes. Reduce the heat to low and simmer for 20 minutes.

Add the washed spinach, which will cook down in minutes, and simmer the soup for another 5 minutes. By this time, the flesh of the fish should be falling off the bone and the soup should be an opaque white color.

To serve, divide the fish, spinach, and carrots between your serving bowls. If you are worried about the bones, you can always strain the soup before serving, pick the fish off the bones, and add it back to the broth.

# PORK OPEN-TOP DUMPLINGS—SIU MAI
# 燒賣

 *Use gluten-free wrappers.*

*Dairy free*

*Egg free*

*Makes approx. 12*

*Preparation time 25 minutes*

*Cooking time 20 minutes*

**7oz ground pork**

**3oz raw, peeled large shrimp,**
**coarsely chopped**

**½ teaspoon salt**

**½ teaspoon sugar**

**pinch of black pepper**

**1 tablespoon potato starch**

**1 drop of sesame oil**

**2 tablespoons water**

**10 dried Chinese mushrooms, soaked**
**in boiling water for 15 minutes**
**then finely chopped**

**1 teaspoon dried finely grated**
**orange peel**

**12 wonton skins, corners trimmed**
**so they are roughly circular**

**\*Lisa's tips**

*Before steaming, oil the plate with a dab*
*of vegetable oil and set each* siu mai *apart*
*from one another, otherwise they will stick*
*together when they steam and cook.*

Our grandmother, Lily, loved joining her father when he went off to sell his soy sauce to the restaurants back in the 1920s. Our great-grandfather made his own cart to transport his barrels of soy sauce; it was heavy yet functional and pulled by him and Lily, who ran alongside her father tantalized by the blur of lights, shapes, people, and noise. When they finally arrived at their destination, she was often treated to free *siu mai*, which she gladly accepted, calling it "a little piece of Heaven" because the meat, Chinese mushrooms, and delicate pastry were so delicious.

I love *siu mai* and this is my own personal take, adapted from the recipe of the Hong Kong chef who trained me. Use crab roe to garnish for the ultimate luxury, although if you are just making these for a weeknight dinner you can use finely grated carrot.

METHOD

Put the ground pork and chopped shrimp in a bowl and mash together with a spoon until well blended. (Don't use a food processor for this because you still want to retain some texture.) Add the salt, sugar, pepper, potato starch, sesame oil, and water and continue to lightly mash the ingredients together. Finally add the chopped Chinese mushrooms and orange peel, mixing well. The mixture is ready when everything is well blended and the mixture sticks to the spoon.

To assemble the dumplings, take one trimmed wonton skin and place it into a cupped hand. Scoop 1 tablespoon of the filling into the wonton skin. Move the dumpling between the thumb and index finger and continue scooping in more filling until it appears full. Begin to turn the dumpling using your thumb and index finger and mold it into the *siu mai* shape. Repeat with the remaining skins.

Lightly oil a heatproof plate and arrange the *siu mai* on top. To cook the *siu mai*, carefully place the plate of dumplings inside a preheated steamer and steam for 15 minutes. (If you don't have a steamer, you can use a wok instead, see page 127.)

# CRISPY WONTONS
# 香雲吞

*Use gluten-free wrappers.*

*Dairy free*

*Egg free*

*Serves 2 (Makes approx. 20)*

*Preparation time 25 minutes*

*Cooking time 10 minutes*

**7oz raw, peeled large shrimp,
   finely chopped**

**7oz ground pork**

**½ teaspoon salt**

**½ teaspoon sugar**

**½ teaspoon sesame oil**

**1 tablespoon potato starch**

**2 tablespoons water**

**20 wonton skins**

**vegetable oil, for deep-frying**

**sweet and sour sauce, to serve**

   *(see page 14)*

**\*Lisa's tips**

*These can be made in advance and
frozen separately.*

Go to a Chinese restaurant on a Sunday afternoon and you will be greeted by a sea of Chinese families spanning three generations. Dim sum is the Chinese equivalent of French hors d'oeuvres or Spanish tapas. It's a colorful and loud dining experience starting with the rush for vacant seats and the hustle and bustle of the gesticulating waiters selling specials from their carts. Bamboo containers filled with steamed dim sum are stacked high and quickly snapped up. Waiting staff ask what kind of tea you want to drink, offering a vast array of teas—jasmine, Oolong, Pu'er, and green—which helps to wash down the dim sum and aids digestion.

Dim sum is an overwhelming introduction to the Chinese nation's love of food, gregariousness, and cheerful chatter. There are over 2,000 dishes to choose from. The range of cooking skills required to make dim sum is immense. There is usually a dim sum master overseeing their section of the kitchen and there is real art involved in making the dishes. Some dishes are steamed, others are fried, and some are baked. The variety of tastes is also mind-boggling: sweet, sour, savory, bitter, spicy, and umami.

These are one of my favorite dim sum. You can fill the wontons with any filling of your choice. I prefer using shrimp as it makes the wontons light when fried. I like to add a flamboyant tail to the pastry, which can then be dipped in the sweet and sour sauce.

METHOD

Put the shrimp and ground pork in a bowl and season with salt, sugar, and sesame oil. Add the potato starch and water and mash well with a fork until well blended—you're looking for the texture of a sticky paste with some texture.

Put 1 teaspoon of the filling into the center of each wonton skin. Using your index finger, dampen one corner of the skin and fold over into a triangle. To seal the edges, pleat them together to give a wavy edge (see photos opposite).

To cook the wontons, fill a wok with approx. ½ cup vegetable oil and preheat over medium heat to 350°F. To test the temperature, see page 35. Lower the wontons into the hot oil and deep-fry for 5 minutes until golden brown. Drain on paper towels and serve with sweet and sour sauce.

# DEEP-FRYING

Many Chinese recipes are deep-fried, but the question I am often asked is how hot should the oil be?
Sometimes you can feel the heat radiate from the wok, but does that mean it is hot enough?
Here are some tips:

If you can see smoke, the oil is too hot—your food will burn quickly on the outside and could end
up raw in the center.
If the oil is too cool, the food will soak up the oil like a sponge and it will turn out greasy.
For most of the recipes in this book, the oil should be at 350°F. If you don't have a thermometer, here
is a simple test. Take an unpainted, natural bamboo chopstick and dip it into the oil. If it bubbles
rapidly around the chopstick end in the oil, then the oil is hot enough for deep-frying. At this stage
reduce the heat to low.

# CRISPY MINI SPRING ROLLS
## 春卷

*Replace the wrappers with rice paper wrappers and glue together with water.*

*Dairy free*

*Egg free*

*Makes approx. 15–20 spring rolls*

*Preparation time 20 minutes*

*Cooking time 20 minutes*

1 medium carrot, peeled and cut
   into julienne strips

1 x 8oz can of bamboo shoot strips

2 tablespoons vegetable oil, plus
   extra for deep-frying

1 medium onion, finely sliced

14oz (4 cups) fresh bean sprouts

½ teaspoon salt

1 teaspoon sugar

½ teaspoon five spice powder

½ teaspoon sesame oil

1 x 8oz pack of 3 x 3-inch spring roll
   wrappers

2 tablespoons flour and
   4 tablespoons cold water,
   mixed to a paste

sweet and sour or sweet chile sauce,
   to serve *(see page 14)*

**\*Lisa's tips**

*Spring rolls freeze well—just make sure you freeze them separately to prevent them from sticking together. (Note that gluten-free rice paper wrappers cannot be frozen).*

I remember learning a fascinating ancient story at Chinese school about how the spring roll became the most popular appetizer on Chinese restaurant menus around the world. Many centuries ago in ancient China, teahouses would prepare a special dish to celebrate the spring festival. This began life as a spring pancake, but as people became wealthier the pancake was replaced by a spring roll, which resembled a gold bar, as this represented their increasing status and power. Today we eat spring rolls during Chinese New Year celebrations to symbolize a prosperous New Year.

METHOD

First blanch the carrots and bamboo shoots. Bring some water to a boil in a wok, drop in the carrot strips and bamboo shoots, and cook for 5 minutes until soft. Drain well, discarding the water, and set aside.

Return the wok to the heat, add the oil and stir-fry the onion and bean sprouts over high heat for 5 minutes. Add the blanched vegetables, season with salt, sugar, five spice powder, and sesame oil, and mix well. Tip the contents of the wok into a colander and set aside to drain; the filling needs to be as dry as possible. Leave to cool.

Separate the spring roll sheets and prepare the flour-water paste—it should be sticky, not runny. To assemble the spring rolls, place a sheet on a flat surface or plate with one corner facing you—i.e. so it forms a diamond. Place 1 tablespoon of the filling in the middle of the spring roll sheet. Bring the corner nearest to you over the filling. Dab some of the flour-water paste onto the left and right corners. Fold the right-hand side over the middle, followed by the left-hand side. Keeping the filling tightly packed, roll the spring roll away from you to form a tight roll. Dab the corner farthest away from you with a little flour and water paste, roll the spring roll away from you, and your spring roll is complete. Repeat with the remaining pastry and filling.

To cook the spring rolls, fill a wok with approx. 1 cup vegetable oil and preheat over medium heat to 350°F. To test the temperature, see page 35. Deep-fry the spring rolls for 5 minutes in the hot oil, turning constantly so the entire spring roll becomes golden like those gold bars! Cook them in batches of 6–8 depending on the size of the pan. Drain on paper towels.

Serve with sweet chile sauce or sweet and sour sauce.

# BEIJING JIAOZI PORK DUMPLINGS
## 北京餃子

Use gluten-free flour rather than all-purpose flour.

Dairy free

Egg free

Serves 2 (Makes approx. 28)

Preparation time 30 minutes

Cooking time 15 minutes

**For the pastry**

**1²⁄₃ cups all-purpose flour, plus extra for dusting**

**½ cup boiling water**

*For the filling*

**7oz ground pork**

**10 stalks of chives or 1 Napa cabbage leaf, finely shredded**

**½ teaspoon salt**

**½ teaspoon sugar**

**1 tablespoon potato starch**

**1 drop of sesame oil**

**2 tablespoons water**

**½ teaspoon Shaoxing rice wine**

*For the dip*

**2 tablespoons red wine vinegar**

**½-inch piece of fresh ginger, peeled and finely sliced**

*Lisa's tips

You can use any type of protein you want for these dumplings, including shrimp, chicken, tofu, or lamb.

To celebrate and bestow prosperity, these dumplings are traditionally cooked for Chinese New Year to symbolize the golden ingots used during the Ming Dynasty. It is entirely up to you what type of filling you want to use, but this is our version that we cook at home and serve at Sweet Mandarin. We served these during the cook-off stages as part of the *F Word* Best Local Chinese Restaurant competition with Gordon Ramsay in 2009.

METHOD

First make the dumpling dough. Put the flour in a deep bowl and gradually add the boiling water, little by little, stirring with a wooden spoon until well blended. Turn out the dough onto a floured surface and knead for 10 minutes. The best technique is to use the palm of your hand to push the dough away from you and then fold in the left and right sides of the dough to the center. Return the dough to the bowl, cover with a damp cloth, and set aside to rest while you make the filling.

To make the filling, combine the pork with the chives or Napa cabbage leaf in a bowl. Add the salt, sugar, potato starch, sesame oil, water, and Shaoxing wine, and mash well with a metal spoon until well blended. The filling is ready when everything is combined and the mixture sticks to the spoon.

Divide the dough into 4 pieces. Roll out each piece of dough into a sausage shape, approx. 8 inches long, and cut into 1-inch small, even-sized stumps. Push down each stump to flatten it with the palm of your hand and use a floured rolling pin to roll it out into a circle. If you wish, you can use a glass (with a diameter of approx. 2 inches) to trim the pastry into nice circles.

To assemble the Beijing dumplings, take one circle of dough in the palm of your hand and scoop 1 tablespoon of the filling into the middle. Dab your index finger into some cold water and wet one side of the dough. Fold the dough over the filling and start closing the dumpling by pinching the sides together to form a half-moon shape. Repeat with the remaining dough.

To cook the dumplings, heat some boiling water in a wok, drop in the dumplings, and cook for 10 minutes. Meanwhile, make the vinegar dip by pouring the vinegar into a little bowl and floating the finely sliced pieces of raw ginger in it.

# COCONUT SHRIMP
# 椰子大蝦

🌾 *Gluten free*

♥ *Dairy free*

*Serves 2 (Makes 10–16)*

*Preparation time 10 minutes*

*Cooking time 5 minutes*

**8oz raw, peeled deveined, large
shrimp, tails intact**

**½ teaspoon salt**

**1 egg, beaten**

**1 cup dried coconut**

**vegetable oil, for deep-frying**

**1¼ cups sweet chile sauce, to serve**

*(see page 14)*

## *Lisa's tips

*This is a great dish for a party. You can batter the shrimp in advance and freeze them until needed. When the party starts, deep-fry the shrimp. Once deep-fried the shrimp cannot be frozen.*

I was working as a corporate lawyer for Clifford Chance in Hong Kong in 2002, and it gave Lisa an excuse to join me for a few weeks. One of the perks was access to the company junk (a Chinese boat), which gave us the opportunity to visit Lamma Island. Famous for its seafood heritage and its peace and tranquility, Lamma Island was a breath of fresh air away from the skyscrapers and traffic jams of Hong Kong.

I remember it was hot and humid on the day of our visit, so we decided to eat outdoors to try to catch the sea breeze. This is what we ate, served by a scraggly looking man with even more scraggly trousers. The freshly caught shrimp were massive, much bigger than I had ever seen before, and I can still picture the scene as they kept trying to jump out of the wok and into the open fire, only to be skillfully caught by a fat woman with sturdy, dexterous hands. Under the fire, the coconuts were roasted, giving a whiff of toffee as they caramelized. This sophisticated dish was the standout meal for me during that visit, and for days afterwards I raved about my new find and how delicate the flavors were. In addition, I was really pleased because bread crumbs were not used, making this probably one of the tastiest, most gluten-free recipes I know.

METHOD

First cut the shrimp slightly lengthwise to devein, keeping the tail end intact. Rub the salt all over the shrimp.

Dip each shrimp first into the beaten egg and then into the coconut. Repeat the process so the shrimp have a double coating, and shake off any excess coconut.

To cook the shrimp, fill a wok with approx. ½ cup vegetable oil and preheat over medium heat to 350°F. To test the temperature, see page 35. Deep-fry the shrimp in the hot oil for 5 minutes until golden brown. Drain on paper towels and serve with sweet chile sauce.

# LETTUCE WRAPS—SAN CHOY BAU WITH CHICKEN
# 生菜包

*Gluten free*

*Dairy free*

*Egg free*

*Makes 10–12*

*Preparation time 10 minutes*

*Cooking time 10 minutes*

½ iceberg lettuce or 2 small Boston
　lettuces, leaves separated

2 tablespoons vegetable oil

1 x 8oz can of bamboo slices

1 x 8oz can of water chestnuts,
　sliced

1 carrot, peeled and cut into
　small dice

6 Chinese mushrooms, soaked in
　boiling water for 15 minutes
　then cut into small dice

1 cooked chicken boneless chicken
　breast, finely sliced

½ teaspoon salt

½ teaspoon sugar

1¼ cups barbecue sauce
　*(see page 15)*

\*Lisa's tips

*You can include any type of protein and
vegetable you like in your lettuce wrap.*

When I make this dish, I think of our grandfather. Chan grew up well practiced in Kung Fu and also immersed in his family's restaurant business, and one of the things he used to do to amuse himself was to throw the lettuces up in the air and halve them mid-air with a machete. Apparently, the result was much practice and lots of wasted lettuces! While I do not recommend slicing the lettuce that way, I do recommend you try this recipe as the combination of textures, flavors, and colors makes the most delicious and healthy San Choy Bau.

METHOD

Wash the lettuce leaves and pat dry on paper towels.

Add the oil to a hot wok and stir-fry the vegetables and chicken over high heat for 5–8 minutes until the vegetables are soft and the chicken is heated through. Season with salt, sugar and a splash of water.

Divide the mixture between the lettuce leaves, pour in some barbecue sauce, and wrap up to form little parcels.

# SALT AND PEPPER JUICY MUSHROOMS

## 椒鹽蘑菇

*Serves 2*

*Preparation time 10 minutes*

*Cooking time 5 minutes*

**1–2 tablespoons vegetable oil**

**1–2 garlic cloves, finely sliced**

**½ medium onion, diced finely**

**½ green pepper, cut into small dice**

**1 fresh red chile, finely sliced**

**8oz button mushrooms, halved**

**½ teaspoon salt**

**1 teaspoon sugar**

**½ teaspoon five spice powder**

**1 tablespoon Shaoxing rice wine**

**\*Lisa's tips**

*It is important to add the spice mix first, and then the Shaoxing wine. If you add them the other way around, this dish will be grainy and the spice mix will not properly dissolve.*

This recipe might change your life. If you've never tasted mushrooms like this before, I highly recommend you try out our recipe. So many customers have told us this is THE best mushroom dish and they can't get enough of it. Thank you to those customers, however, all we are doing is combining simple ingredients and flavors with a skilful technique.

METHOD

Add the oil to a preheated wok. Quickly stir-fry the garlic, onion, pepper, and chile over high heat for 1 minute.

Add the mushrooms and cook for 4–5 minutes until they are browned. Sprinkle in the salt, sugar, and five spice powder. Add the Shaoxing rice wine and toss well.

# SESAME SHRIMP TOASTIES
## 芝麻蝦多士

🌾 *Use gluten-free bread.*
♥ *Dairy free*
◖ *Egg free*
*Serves 2*
*Preparation time 15 minutes*
*Cooking time 15 minutes*

**5oz raw, peeled large shrimp,**
    **deveined**
**1 teaspoon salt**
**pinch of white pepper**
**1 drop of sesame oil**
**2 slices of thick white bread**
**1/3 cup raw sesame seeds**
**vegetable oil, for deep-frying**
**sweet and sour sauce, to serve**
    *(see page 14)*

**\*Lisa's tips**
*Put the bread in the freezer for 30 minutes*
*beforehand, which will prevent it from*
*breaking up when you spread the shrimp*
*paste on it.*

An old Chinese fable goes that this dish was created by a Beijing chef, whose specialty was mantou bread, and a Guangzhou chef, whose specialty was seafood. The Beijing chef travelled to Guangzhou to visit his friend and together they combined their specialties in one dish. My cooking students have always wondered how shrimp toast is made, and many of them say it is one of their all-time favorite dim sum. The key to the perfect shrimp toast is to ensure the oil is hot enough to fry the shrimp toast without its absorbing the oil. Use raw sesame seeds for a golden shrimp toast; don't use toasted sesame seeds, which will result in blackened seeds once they have been deep-fried.

METHOD
Blend the shrimp in a food processor until smooth. Season with salt, white pepper, and sesame oil.

Spread the shrimp mixture evenly onto one side of the bread, making sure it covers the corners as well.

Pour the sesame seeds onto a plate. Dunk the shrimp-side of the toast into the sesame seeds and press down carefully so that they stick. If necessary, sprinkle some more sesame seeds over the corners.

To cook the shrimp toasts, fill a wok with approx. 2/3 cup vegetable oil and preheat over medium heat to 350°F. To test the temperature, see page 35. Carefully lower the shrimp toasts into the hot oil, shrimp-side down, and hold down under the surface to stop them from floating. Deep-fry the toasts for 4–5 minutes or until they turn golden brown, are crisp on both sides, and the shrimp topping is completely cooked through. Once cooked, the shrimp paste will turn opaque and the sesame seeds will darken to a light golden brown. Remove the toasts with a slotted spoon and drain on paper towels.

To serve, cut the shrimp toasts into quarters and accompany with sweet and sour sauce.

# SALT AND CHILE SQUID
# 椒鹽鮮魷

 Gluten free

 Dairy free

Serves 2

Preparation time 10 minutes

Cooking time 15 minutes

5oz squid tubes, scored with a
   lattice pattern and cut into
   1-inch slices

1 teaspoon salt, plus extra for
   sprinkling

1 egg, beaten

5 tablespoons potato starch or
   cornstarch, for coating

1 teaspoon vegetable oil, plus extra
   for deep-frying

1–2 garlic cloves, minced or sliced

½ onion, finely diced

½ green pepper, cut into ¼-inch dice

1 fresh red chile, thinly sliced

¼ teaspoon five spice powder

½ teaspoon sugar

2 tablespoons Shaoxing rice wine

*Lisa's tips

*Scoring the squid helps reduce its tendency
to curl up. The best way is to cut the tubes
into 1-inch slices, open them out flat, and
score the inside with a lattice pattern.*

We cooked this dish for the final of Gordon Ramsay's *F Word* Best Local Chinese Restaurant in the UK in 2009. I finished service at Sweet Mandarin at midnight and after just two hours of sleep we were picked up by a SHINY black car and driven to a secret destination in London. We were whisked into a fancy kitchen with a boiling hot Aga and told we had just one hour to prepare our squid for 50 people.

Our Salt and Chile Squid was one of three dishes that helped us win the competition. As we raised the trophy, I swear I could hear the *Rocky IV* theme tune "Eye of the Tiger" belting out.

This simple recipe combines contrasting textures and is packed full of flavor. Squid can so easily be overcooked and rubbery, but if you follow our steps you'll be sure to serve the best cooked squid!

METHOD

Sprinkle a pinch of salt over the squid pieces and dip them first into the beaten egg and then into the potato starch or cornstarch.

To cook the squid, fill a wok with approx. ²/₃ cup oil and preheat over medium heat to 350°F*. To test the temperature, see page 35. Lower the squid into the hot oil and deep-fry for 5–7 minutes until they curl up and are nicely crisp. Drain on paper towels and set aside.

Heat a clean wok, add 1 teaspoon of vegetable oil, and quickly stir-fry the garlic, onion, pepper, and chile over high heat for 3 minutes. Put in the deep-fried squid pieces and cook for 2–3 minutes, stirring. Sprinkle in the five spice powder, 1 teaspoon of salt, and the sugar. Add the Shaoxing wine and toss well to combine.

*Note:* If you don't want to deep-fry the squid, simply stir-fry the raw squid (without the egg and potato starch batter) in a hot wok with 1 tablespoon of vegetable oil. Drain on paper towels and set aside.

# HAWKER-STALL–STYLE CHICKEN SKEWERS WITH SATAY DIP
## 串燒雞肉沙嗲

*Use tamari rather than soy sauce.*

*Dairy free*

*Egg free*

*Serves 2*

*Preparation time 30 minutes*

*Cooking time 15 minutes*

**7oz boneless chicken breasts, cut into 4-inch strips**

*For the marinade*

**1 tablespoon sesame oil**

**1 tablespoon Shaoxing rice wine or sherry**

**1 tablespoon light soy sauce**

**½ teaspoon salt**

**½ teaspoon sugar**

**½ teaspoon minced garlic**

*For the satay dip*

**1 cup raw, unsalted peanuts**

**1 tablespoon brown sugar**

**½ teaspoon salt**

**½ teaspoon ground turmeric**

**½ teaspoon chile paste**

**2 tablespoons water**

**1 tablespoon vegetable oil**

**\*Lisa's tips**

*These can either be cooked in the oven, on a grill pan, or over a barbecue.*

Hong Kong was, and still is, famous for its amazing range of culinary offerings. As Chinese immigrants poured into Hong Kong to escape the Japanese invasion of China during the 1920s, the streets boasted increasing numbers of restaurants and street hawker stalls known as *dai pai dongs*. Although the *dai pai dongs* were no more than tiny metal carts, they served up a wide array of street foods—including these chicken skewers, as well as other snacks such as pungent preserved beancurd, fishballs, and Shanghai dumplings called potstickers because they stuck to the pot. One of the reasons the *dai pai dongs* were so successful was because the vendors had the foresight to put most of their items on a stick, making eating on the go possible. The rise in foodsellers reduced prices and made food available to the masses. These foodsellers could be found throughout the city and turned snacking into a Chinese institution. If you had the appetite, you could eat from morning until midnight. Chicken skewers with peanut satay dip became a firm favorite with the nation.

METHOD

Soak 12 wooden skewers, approx. 7 inches in length, in warm water for 30 minutes. Cut the chicken into 4-inch long strips.

Meanwhile, mix together the ingredients for the marinade in a bowl. Put in the chicken strips, coat them well on all sides, and set aside to marinate for at least 20 minutes.

Prepare the satay dip by crushing the peanuts using a mortar and pestle (or put them in a plastic bag and crush with a rolling pin). You want to retain some texture in the sauce so it is not advisable to blend the peanuts in a food processor. Tip the crushed peanuts into a saucepan (without any oil) and toast them over low heat until they start to brown, approx. 3 minutes. Stir in the sugar, salt, turmeric, chile paste, water, and oil and cook for 5 minutes. Set aside.

Preheat a grill pan. Thread the marinated chicken strips onto the wooden skewers and cook for approx. 3 minutes on each side or until golden brown and cooked through. Serve with the satay sauce.

Poultry and eggs are a weekly staple in our shopping basket. These everyday ingredients are the backbone of family meals, and the recipes in this chapter range from quick and easy stir-fries to labors of love such as Cantonese Roast Chicken. Chinese cooks tend to use all parts of the chicken and none of it is wasted. For convenience, however, the majority of these recipes use boneless chicken breasts.

Poultry features in Chinese weddings as a key part of traditional culture. Dishes using poultry are referred to as the "Phoenix" and seafood dishes are the "Dragon." The combination of the two represents a good marriage and a happy family for the future. Poultry recipes are also cooked during other Chinese celebrations, such as Chinese New Year, to bless the year ahead with good fortune. Egg dishes symbolize fertility and are often eaten after the birth of a new baby.

In this chapter, the standout dish, and our mother's favorite recipe, is Mabel's Clay Pot Chicken, a twice-cooked casserole with chicken, Chinese mushrooms, which have an earthy, woody taste, *lap cheong* (Chinese sausage), which adds an intensely sweet, smoked flavor, and bok choy, which brings a modicum of lightness to the clay pot. We cooked this dish for Gordon Ramsay on the *F Word* and won the Best Local Chinese Restaurant, beating 10,000 other restaurants to this amazing accolade. We hope you enjoy our mother's dish as much as Gordon Ramsay did.

# 家禽和雞蛋

# POULTRY
# & EGGS

# THE ULTIMATE CHICKEN FOO YUNG
# 雞芙蓉蛋

*Gluten free*

*Dairy free*

*Serves 2*

*Preparation time 10 minutes*

*Cooking time 15 minutes*

**2 tablespoons vegetable oil**

**4oz (1 cup) bean sprouts**

**4oz (½ cup) green beans, cut into 1-inch lengths**

**1 medium onion, finely sliced**

**1½ cups thinly sliced cooked chicken breast**

**pinch of salt**

**4 large eggs, beaten**

***Lisa's tips**

*This can be made with any filling of your choice, such as shrimp, beef, pork, or vegetables.*

*The trick to making the perfect Chinese omelette is to ensure that the oil is smoking hot. The eggs will sizzle when they hit the pan and give the omelette a crispy edge.*

Foo Yung has been criticized for being an anglicized Chinese dish, but actually this omelette dish has roots in a Shanghainese dish called Fu Yung Egg Slices. During the early 1950s it was estimated that there were 5,000 Chinese people based in British ports, many of them working in launderettes. When the domestic washing machine was invented, many businesses became redundant, and some Chinese were forced to turn their hands to other trades—including a certain Mr. Foo, who converted his launderette into a take-out restaurant. The only problem was that Mr. Foo was a hopeless cook; he couldn't tell the difference between green beans and onions, and he had no idea of measurements. When a customer asked for an onion omelette, Mr. Foo threw in green beans and onions in the hope that one would be the right ingredient and poured in too much egg. The customer was thrilled and ordered it again and again. By the time the laundry man had realized his mistake, it was too late; the humble Foo Yung was born and it made its way onto the menu permanently. Twenty years after this incident, the number of Chinese immigrants increased tenfold, with nearly all of them working in catering and offering Foo Yung on their menus.

This dish has always proved really popular in our family take-out restaurant. Many of our regulars order the same dish at the same time every week and this includes Jerry, who has been ordering this dish for decades. So here, Jerry, is the ultimate Chicken Foo Yung for you.

METHOD

Add 1 tablespoon of oil to a hot wok. Put in the vegetables and chicken and stir-fry for 5 minutes over high heat until the chicken is heated through. Season with a pinch of salt. Tip the contents of the wok into a colander and drain well to remove excess moisture.

Clean the wok, return it to high heat, and add another tablespoon of oil. Return the vegetables and chicken to the wok. Pour the beaten eggs around the vegetables and chicken and cook for 5 minutes without stirring. Once the omelette has set, carefully flip it over and cook on the other side for another 5 minutes. Once cooked, the Foo Yung should be the consistency of a firm omelette (rather than soft like scrambled eggs).

Serve with steamed rice—or french fries, as Jerry likes it!

# ADAM AND EVE'S OYSTER OMELETTE
## 蚵仔煎

🌾 *Gluten free*

♥ *Dairy free*

*Serves 2*

*Preparation time 10 minutes*

*Cooking time 10 minutes*

**10 fresh oysters or 1 x 4oz can of
    oysters, drained**

**2 tablespoons vegetable oil**

**4 medium eggs, beaten**

**pinch of salt**

**1 scallion, finely sliced**

**\*Lisa's tips**

*Fresh oysters are best, but a can of oysters
or defrosted frozen oysters also work.*

A dear customer who asked to remain anonymous came to Sweet Mandarin one night with her husband to eat. I will call them Adam and Eve. During their meal, an argument ensued and Adam walked out to cool down. Eve was distraught and, bawling her eyes out on my apron, explained how she desperately wanted children but it just wasn't happening. I told her not to worry and that I had a plan…

When Adam came back, I turned the lights down and lit a candle for the couple. Then I returned to the kitchen and created this dish just for them, knowing that oysters are a natural aphrodisiac (they have high levels of zinc, which boosts the sperm count).

This dish is the perfect marriage of just-cooked-to-perfection oysters and eggs. The oysters' pearly texture contrasts perfectly with egg. This omelette is really quick and easy to make and great if you want to try something different from the usual fillings.

I'm pleased to tell you that Adam and Eve are still married and now have two children. Who knows if this dish was instrumental in their happy ending, but I'd like to think I did my bit as the cupid chef!

METHOD

Carefully open the oyster shells, remove the oysters, and rinse briefly under running water. Drain on paper towels.

Add 1 tablespoon of oil to a hot wok. Put in the oysters and stir-fry for 20 seconds. Add the beaten eggs and cook over high heat without stirring, for 5 minutes until the omelette starts to firm up around the edges. You may need to add a drizzle of oil around the sides to stop the omelette from sticking. Season with a pinch of salt. Carefully flip the omelette over and cook for another 5 minutes on the other side or until the eggs are firm.

Sprinkle on the scallion to serve.

# STEAMED SAVORY EGG WITH CHICKEN, SHRIMP, AND SCALLIONS
## 嫩滑蒸水蛋

🌾 *Use tamari rather than soy sauce.*

♥ *Dairy free*

*Serves 2*

*Preparation time 15 minutes*

*Cooking time 15 minutes*

**2 eggs**

**1 teaspoon salt**

**½ cup boiled and cooled water**

**¾ cup cooked chicken, cut into thin strips**

**6 raw, peeled large shrimp, cut into thirds**

**1 scallion, finely sliced**

**1 tablespoon light soy sauce**

### *Lisa's tips

*Using cooled boiled water rather than from the faucet makes the egg smoother in consistency.*

*Use ramekins with sides no higher than 3 inches to ensure that the egg is properly cooked through.*

You've had fried eggs, boiled eggs, poached eggs, and scrambled eggs, but there is one more way that the Chinese love to eat eggs, and that is steamed. This dish is perfect for breakfast, and it was a firm favorite with our grandmother who used to enjoy it after her Tai Chi exercises at 5 a.m.

This recipe is one our grandmother made for our mother, and our mother used to make for us. The dish is made by mixing water and egg together and steaming it to create a texture similar to silken tofu. The soft texture and saltiness of the chicken and shrimp make it perfect for eating with steamed boiled rice.

METHOD

Beat the eggs in a bowl, add the salt and water, and continue to beat until thoroughly combined. Pour the mixture into two ramekins and divide the chicken, shrimp, and scallion between them.

Heat a steamer, put in the ramekins, and cover with a lid. If you don't have a steamer, you can always use a wok filled with hot water (see page 127). Steam the eggs for 10 minutes over medium heat before checking to see if the egg is set. If it is still wobbly in the center, steam for another 5 minutes.

Once cooked, remove the ramekins from the steamer and drizzle on the soy sauce. Serve with some steamed rice on the side.

# SHRIMP WITH TOMATOES AND EGG
## 大蝦番茄炒蛋

*Gluten free*

*Dairy free*

*Serves 2*

*Preparation time 10 minutes*

*Cooking time 15 minutes*

**1 tablespoon vegetable oil**

**1 garlic clove, minced**

**1 medium onion, finely sliced**

**14 medium raw, peeled shrimp,**
   **deveined**

**2 medium tomatoes, quartered**

**²⁄₃ cup chicken or vegetable stock**
   *(see pages 12–13)*

**2 tablespoons ketchup**

**½ teaspoon salt**

**1 teaspoon sugar**

**1 tablespoon potato starch mixture**
   *(see page 8)*

**1 egg, beaten**

**\*Lisa's tips**

*Remove the wok from the heat when you add the egg so it cooks gently in a boiling sauce and doesn't scramble. To create the egg swirls, swirl the beaten egg into circles using a fork once you've added it to the hot soup.*

I was very insecure when I was a child and hated the fact that I was Chinese and had a flat nose. In fact, after studying Louisa May Alcott's *Little Women* at school, I actually slept for a while with a peg on my nose in the hope that it would turn out straighter like my schoolfriends'—however, every morning it was flat as a button. As I grew up, I realized that my dual culture is actually an asset and not something to be hidden. We worked in the family take-out restaurant, and I became proud of the fact that I could cook the entire menu by the time I was 11. This dish takes me back to my childhood, when Dad used to make us this for Friday dinner after the busy rush of customers had subsided. I particularly love the egg swirls in the tomato sauce, although I prefer my own version these days because it has lots of delicious sauce to go with the rice! This is my idea of comfort food.

METHOD

Heat the wok until it is just starting to smoke. Add the oil and swirl it around in the wok. Add the garlic and onion and stir-fry for 2 minutes. Throw in the shrimp and cook for 5 minutes, tossing well until they are cooked through.

Add the tomatoes and cook for 2 minutes, stirring. Pour in the stock and stir well. Add the ketchup, salt, and sugar and taste to check the seasoning.

Bring the sauce to a boil and add the potato starch mixture, stirring vigorously until it thickens.

Remove the wok from the heat and swirl in 3 tablespoons of the beaten egg. Return the wok to the heat to set the egg, which will contrast beautifully with the red tomatoes. Serve with steamed rice.

# MOM'S FAVORITE SALTED DUCK EGGS
# 鹹鴨蛋

*Gluten free*

*Dairy free*

*Makes 12 eggs*

*Preparation time 15 minutes*

*Soaking time 30–40 days*

**12 duck eggs or hen eggs**

**3¾ cups water**

**⅔ cup sea salt or rock salt**

**1 star anise**

**2 teaspoons Szechuan peppercorns**

**1 tablespoon Shaoxing rice wine**

**\*Lisa's tips**

*Use in casseroles, omelettes, or fried rice to add salty flavor and texture.*

As a child I remember seeing these bright white eggs in the carton and wondering what was different about them. When my mother told me to try one, I remember making a face and asking why they were so salty. Mom said they were a Chinese specialty known as Salted Duck Eggs, and the best ones had bright, orangey yolks and translucent whites. Over the years I've grown to love them, and I could happily eat one or two whole salty eggs on my own, with steamed rice on the side. Why don't you give them a try? They will change your perspective on normal boiled eggs forever.

METHOD

Rinse the eggs and dry carefully on paper towels; set aside.

Pour the water into a saucepan and season with the salt, star anise, and Szechuan peppercorns. Bring to a boil, stirring until the salt dissolves, and then remove from the heat. Set aside to cool completely.

Once cold, pour in the wine and stir well. Carefully arrange the eggs in a 2-quart clean glass container. Check every egg to make sure there are no cracks. Pour the cold, salty water over the eggs. You'll notice some eggs will float to the surface, so place something, like a saucer or plate, on top to keep them submerged. Tightly cover the container with plastic wrap and set aside at room temperature for 30–40 days. Label the start and finish dates on the container to remind yourself.

Drain the eggs and dry them carefully with paper towels. Put them in an egg carton and store in the fridge. The salted eggs will keep for up to 4 weeks in the fridge.

# PEKING DUCKENAIL *(Duck, chicken, and quail roast)*
# 鴨雞鵪鶉

- Gluten free
- Dairy free
- Egg free

Serves 2

Preparation time 25 minutes

Cooking time 1¼ hours

**For the plum sauce**

3 plums, peeled, pitted, and
    quartered

½ red chile, sliced into small pieces

3 tablespoons sugar

½ teaspoon five spice powder

1 teaspoon white vinegar

¼ cup water

**For the stuffing**

2oz cooked chestnuts, chopped

2oz dried shiitake mushrooms,
    soaked in hot water for 15
    minutes then cut into small pieces

½ cup sticky rice *(see page 168)*

1oz Chinese sausage (lap cheong),
    cut into ¼-inch dice

1 teaspoon salt

1 teaspoon sugar

½ teaspoon five spice powder

½ teaspoon garlic powder

2 teaspoons sesame oil

1 teaspoon Shaoxing rice wine

2 boneless duck breasts, skin on

2 teaspoons salt

1 teaspoon five spice powder

2 chicken thighs, boned and skin
    removed

2 quail filets, boned and skin
    removed

While I love the flavors of Peking Duck, it is very difficult to recreate in the home kitchen—that is what inspired me to create this dish. This is a unique family roast comprised of a quail in a chicken in a duck stuffed with a mix of Chinese mushrooms, chestnuts, Chinese sausage, and sticky rice. We invented it as an alternative Christmas dinner, Chinese-style, and it came about because my sister Janet wanted quail, Lisa wanted duck, and I wanted chicken. So we thought, why not put them all together? It started off as a bit of a challenge, and a bit tongue in cheek, but the end product was such a hit we now enjoy it at other times of the year, too. For Christmas, we used a whole duck, a whole chicken, and a whole quail. However, I have adapted our family recipe for two people rather than for a family of six.

METHOD

Preheat the oven to 450°F.

To make the plum sauce, put all the ingredients in a saucepan and bring to a boil. Reduce the heat and simmer until the plums soften to a pulp. Remove from the heat and set aside to cool.

To prepare the stuffing, put all the ingredients in a bowl and mix well until they bind together. Divide the mixture into six equal portions.

To prepare the duckenail parcels, rub the skin of each duck breast with 1 teaspoon of salt and ½ teaspoon of five spice powder. Arrange the duck breasts, skin-side down, on two squares of foil. Spread one portion of stuffing over each duck breast.

Using a rolling pin, pound each chicken thigh so it is approx. 1 inch thick all over. Place on top of the stuffing. Top with another layer of stuffing. Arrange the quail on top, and cover with the remaining stuffing. Roll the duckenail parcels up inside the foil to create a tight roll.

To cook the duckenail, put the foil parcels on a baking sheet and roast in the hot oven for 30 minutes. Then remove the foil, reduce the temperature to 425°F and continue to cook for another 30 minutes. To crisp up the skin, put the parcels under a moderate broiler for 5–10 minutes.

To serve, carve the meat and accompany with the plum sauce.

# AROMATIC CRISPY DUCK
# 香酥鴨

**11oz duck legs, skin on**

**cornstarch, for dusting**

**vegetable oil, for deep-frying**

*For the marinade*

**1 tablespoon Szechuan peppercorns**

**1 teaspoon five spice powder**

**2 star anise**

**1 teaspoon salt**

**1 tablespoon Shaoxing rice wine**

**1 teaspoon dark soy sauce**

**¾ cup water**

*For the crepes*

**1¾ cups flour**

**½ teaspoon salt**

**¾ cup boiling water**

**sesame oil, for brushing**

*To serve*

**1 cucumber, cut into thin 3-inch sticks**

**4 scallions, white part only, cut into 3-inch lengths then quartered**

**hoisin sauce**

Aromatic crispy duck is the our answer to Peking Duck; the latter originated during the Yuan Dynasty and appeared on imperial court menus for the Emperor of China. Imperial chefs were sworn to secrecy and the recipe wasn't revealed until after the Republic of China was born in 1912, when the head chef started creating Peking Duck for the masses.

METHOD

Score the duck skin all over in a criss-cross pattern and dust with cornstarch. Combine the ingredients for the marinade in a saucepan and bring to a boil. Add the duck and simmer for 20 minutes until cooked through. Remove the pan from the heat and set aside to marinate for 1 hour.

While the duck is marinating, make the crepes. Combine the flour, salt, and boiling water in a bowl, and mix together with a fork until the ingredients start to come together. Use your hands to bring the dough into a ball, and then transfer onto a floured work surface. Knead the dough for 5 minutes until smooth, adding a little more water or flour if necessary. Return the dough to the bowl, cover with a damp towel, and set aside to rest at room temperature for 30 minutes.

Remove the duck legs from the marinade and pat dry on paper towels. Transfer them to a plate and set aside to dry in the fridge, uncovered, for 10 minutes.

Now your dough is ready to use. Transfer onto a lightly floured surface and knead until smooth but not sticky. Roll out into a large rectangle, and cut out small circles approx. 2½ inches in diameter—I use a large cup as a guide. Using a pastry brush, brush a light coating of sesame oil over both sides of the dough circles.

To cook the crepes, pan-fry for 1–2 minutes on each side. Once cooked, layer the crepes on a plate and cover with foil to keep warm.

Heat 3 cups vegetable oil over high heat to 350°F and test the temperature (see page 35). Deep-fry the duck for 8–10 minutes until it turns dark brown. Remove the crispy duck with a slotted spoon and drain on paper towels, patting it dry. Transfer the duck to a plate, and shred the flesh with two forks.

Serve with the crepes, cucumber, scallions, and hoisin sauce.

# SWEET MANDARIN'S SWEET CHILE CHICKEN THIGHS
## 甜辣醬雞腿

*Gluten free*

*Dairy free*

*Egg free*

*Serves 2*

*Preparation time 5 minutes*

*Cooking time 30 minutes*

**2 tablespoons vegetable oil**

**1 onion, finely chopped**

**14oz chicken thighs (approx.
4 thighs)**

**1¼ cups sweet chile sauce**
*(see page 14)*

**¼ cup chicken stock** *(see page 12)*

**3 small mixed peppers (red, yellow,
and green), finely sliced**

**＊Lisa's tips**

*Chicken thigh meat has a deeper flavor
than breast meat that complements the
sweet chile perfectly. However, you can
also use chicken breasts for this recipe if
you wish.*

Our grandmother told me she created sweet chile sauce by pure accident one day when she grabbed the sugar instead of the salt. She was working for a British family in Hong Kong back in the 1950s at the time and was summoned to the dining room afterward, where the head of the household informed her that the sauce was sweet not salty, as instructed. "I thought that was the end of me," she said. Surprisingly for Lily, he was impressed and wanted to know its name. She replied, in surprise "Sweet? Chile?" And the head of the household answered "Very well, Lily, get us some more of this sweet chile."

We followed our grandmother's recipe to make our own Sweet Mandarin Sweet Chile Dipping Sauce, and we think the fact that it is a bestseller is due to our use of fresh chiles. It's a family favorite and hopefully will become one of yours, too.

METHOD

Add the oil to a hot wok. Add the onion and stir-fry over high heat for 5 minutes until soft and translucent.

Add the chicken thighs, skin-side down, and cook for 10 minutes. Turn the chicken thighs over and cook for another 5–7 minutes on the other side until almost cooked through.

Meanwhile, pour the sweet chile sauce into a saucepan and simmer for 5–7 minutes. Set aside.

Pour the chicken stock into the wok with the chicken thighs and bring to a boil. Add the sliced peppers and simmer gently for 2 minutes. Before serving, check that the chicken thighs are fully cooked by poking a knife into the thickest part of the chicken; the juices should run clear.

To serve, spoon the peppers onto a plate, arrange the thighs on top, and spoon on the warm sweet chile sauce.

# MR. CHOW'S OVEN-BAKED BARBECUE CHICKEN WINGS
## 燒烤雞翅

*Gluten free*

*Dairy free*

*Egg free*

*Serves 2*

*Preparation time 5 minutes*

*Cooking time 20 minutes*

**1¾ lbs chicken wings**

**1¼ cups barbecue sauce**

   *(see page 15)*

**3 scallions, finely sliced**

\*Lisa's tips

*If you don't have time to make the barbecue sauce  you can use a store-bought variety. Our Sweet Mandarin Barbecue Sauce doesn't need overnight marinating. This sauce works beautifully with any meats in the oven.*

"I can still taste those barbecue chicken wings from old Mr. Chow on the corner of Stanley market," said our grandmother. "They were the first thing your grandfather bought for me on our first meeting in Hong Kong. He also had to buy a portion for my friend, Kat. In those days, you couldn't go on a date un-chaperoned."

It turns out that right after that date, our grandmother set about experimenting with the herbs and spices in her employer's well-stocked kitchen to replicate the taste of love that she had experienced on that starry night in Stanley.

Unlike other barbecue sauces, our Sweet Mandarin Barbecue Dipping Sauce doesn't require any marinating at all. It is literally packed with herbs and spices to bring the chicken wings to life—and hopefully it will bring your love life to life, too!

METHOD

Preheat the oven to 400°F.

Wash the chicken wings under running water, drain well, and pat dry on paper towels.

Lay the chicken wings on a foil-lined baking sheet, and pour on the barbecue sauce. Ensure all of the chicken is evenly covered.

Roast the chicken wings in the hot oven for 20 minutes.

Remove the chicken wings from the oven and scatter the scallions over the top to serve.

# CHICKEN WITH CHINESE MUSHROOMS *(Women's Day Casserole)*

## 冬菇炆雞

○ *Use tamari rather than oyster sauce and soy sauce.*

♡ *Dairy free*

◯ *Egg free*

*Serves 2*

*Preparation time 10 minutes*

*Cooking time 35 minutes*

2 tablespoons vegetable oil

3 thin slices of fresh ginger

1 garlic clove, sliced

8oz boneless chicken thighs,
   cut into bite-sized pieces

10 dried Chinese mushrooms

2 scallions, cut into 1-inch lengths

2/3 cup water

1/2 teaspoon salt

1/2 teaspoon sugar

1/2 teaspoon sesame oil

1 teaspoon oyster sauce

1/2 teaspoon Shaoxing rice wine

1 tablespoon light soy sauce

2 tablespoons potato starch mixture
   *(see page 8)*

**\*Lisa's tips**

*Chinese mushrooms have a delicious umami flavor, and in their dried form they can last for months. Keep them in your pantry to add to dishes if you want something special.*

The first rally of women under Chinese party leadership was held on Women's Day, March 8, 1924, in Canton, where a group of girl students and women workers raised slogans such as: "Down with imperialism," "Down with warlords," "Same work same pay," "Protection for child labor and pregnant mothers," "Equal education," "Abolish child brides and polygamy," "Prohibit the buying of slave girls and the taking of concubines," and "Formulate a child protection law." These anti-imperialist and anti-feudal slogans echoed throughout the country and ushered in a new phase in the women's movement. These women were instrumental in pairing the ingredients of this dish in honor of former generations who had sacrificed their lives for the cause. The chicken represented the hope of abundance, the reconstituted dried mushrooms symbolized a new beginning, and the use of garlic, ginger, and scallion—China's holy trinity of ingredients—stood for the trinity of the husband, wife, and country.

METHOD

Preheat a large, nonstick saucepan, add the oil, and fry the ginger and garlic for 2 minutes to release their flavor into the oil. Add the chicken and brown for 10 minutes. Throw in the Chinese mushrooms and scallions, and stir-fry for 3 minutes. Pour in the water and add the salt, sugar, sesame oil, oyster sauce, Shaoxing wine, and light soy sauce. Bring to a boil, stirring, cover with a lid, and simmer for 20 minutes.

To thicken the sauce, bring it to a boil, and stir in the potato starch mixture. Serve with jasmine rice.

# GENERAL TSE'S SWEET AND SOUR CHICKEN
## 酸甜雞柳

*Gluten free*

*Dairy free*

*Egg free*

*Serves 2*

*Preparation time 10 minutes*

*Cooking time 30 minutes*

**6oz skinless, boneless chicken breasts, cut into 1-inch cubes**

**½ teaspoon salt**

**½ teaspoon sugar**

**1 tablespoon potato starch, plus extra for coating**

**3 tablespoons water**

**vegetable oil, for deep-frying**

*For the sweet and sour sauce*

**1 teaspoon vegetable oil**

**½ green or red pepper (or a mixture of each), cut into ½-inch dice**

**½ onion, finely chopped**

**⅓ cup pineapple chunks**

**5 tablespoons white sugar**

**2 tablespoons ketchup**

**4 tablespoons white vinegar**

**1¼ cups cold water**

**2 lemon slices**

### *Lisa's tips

*Marinating the chicken with salt, sugar, and potato starch stops it becoming rubbery. You can poach the chicken first, before stir-frying, to ensure that it stays moist and doesn't dry out.*

This dish is renowned all over the world. There is an age-old debate about whether sweet and sour is an authentic Chinese dish or whether it was created to cater for Western palates. In fact, Sweet and Sour Pork originates from the 18th century and was the definitive dish used to test the skills of chefs. In the Guangzhou region, Sweet and Sour Pork is very popular—note its original name was simply Vinegar and Sugar Pork (*tang cu* lǐjǐ). You could say that Sweet and Sour Chicken is its distant relation, although it is slightly sweeter in taste.

This recipe was handed down from our dad, whom we used to call General Tse because he was always giving out orders. This version consists of light, crispy chicken balls tossed in a perfectly balanced sauce, but you could stir-fry the chicken and vegetables together for a healthier dish.

METHOD

Put the chicken in a bowl. Add the salt, sugar, potato starch, and the water and combine well. Cover the bowl with plastic wrap and set aside to marinate in the fridge for 10 minutes.

Meanwhile, fill a wok with approx. ⅔ cup oil and preheat over medium heat to 350°F. Test the temperature with a bamboo chopstick (see page 35).

Remove the chicken from the fridge and dip each piece into potato starch to coat it on all sides. Deep-fry the chicken in the hot oil for 5–6 minutes until golden brown. Remove with a slotted spoon and drain on paper towels. Pour off the oil from the wok into a metal container; this can be reused for cooking.

To make the sauce, return the wok to the heat, add 1 teaspoon of vegetable oil, and stir-fry the peppers, onion, and pineapple over high heat for 3 minutes until the vegetables start to soften. Add the remaining ingredients and bring to a boil. Don't overcook the sauce or it will caramelize and turn black.

Add the cooked pieces of chicken to the bubbling sauce and toss well to coat. Serve with egg-fried rice.

# PENINSULA-STYLE CHICKEN WITH CASHEW NUTS

## 腰果雞丁

*Use tamari rather than oyster and soy sauce.*

*Dairy free*

*Egg free*

*Serves 2*

*Preparation time 10 minutes*

*Cooking time 20 minutes*

**8oz boneless, skinless chicken breast, sliced**

**1 teaspoon salt**

**1½ teaspoons sugar**

**1 tablespoon potato starch**

**3 tablespoons water**

**2 tablespoons vegetable oil**

**1 medium onion, cut into ½-inch dice**

**1 carrot, peeled and cut into fine dice**

**1 scallion, finely sliced**

**⅔ cup chicken stock** *(see page 12)*

**1 tablespoon oyster sauce**

**1 teaspoon Shaoxing rice wine**

**1 teaspoon dark soy sauce**

**1 teaspoon sesame oil**

**1 teaspoon potato starch mixture** *(see page 8)*

**⅔ cup cashew nuts, toasted in a dry frying pan over low heat for 3–5 minutes**

*✱**Lisa's tips***

*Put the roasted cashew nuts in right at the end so that they retain their crunchiness.*

Hong Kong enjoyed some of its best years during the 1920s, an era that saw the building of the famous Peninsula Hotel—a legend of Eastern and Western hospitality, hailed as the Grande Dame of the Far East. According to our grandmother, it was the most amazing building in those days, ideally situated at Tsimshatsui, a prosperous part of the Kowloon peninsula, to take advantage of the Western visitors to the region. The food was luxurious to match the surroundings and included this very popular dish, which would have been very extravagant back then since cashew nuts were relatively rare in those days. Our recipe is fragrant and luxurious in honor of the Peninsula Hotel.

METHOD

Put the chicken in a small bowl with ½ teaspoon of salt, ½ teaspoon of sugar, the potato starch, and water. Set aside to marinate for 10 minutes.

Add 1 tablespoon of oil to a hot wok and stir-fry the chicken for 10 minutes over high heat until cooked through. Remove the chicken from the wok and set aside on a plate. Don't wash the wok because you want to retain the flavors from the chicken.

Put the wok back over high heat and add the remaining oil. Add in the onion, carrot, and scallion and stir-fry for 4 minutes until the onions have softened and browned slightly.

Return the cooked chicken to the pan along with the chicken stock, oyster sauce, ½ teaspoon of salt, 1 teaspoon of sugar, the Shaoxing wine, soy sauce, and sesame oil. Cook for another 5 minutes, stirring, until the stock is bubbling.

Add the potato starch mixture and stir vigorously until the sauce thickens.

Sprinkle with the toasted cashew nuts and toss well to mix. Serve with jasmine rice.

# CHICKEN WITH SWEET PEPPERS AND BLACK BEANS

## 豉椒炒雞柳

- Gluten free
- Dairy free
- Egg free

*Serves 2*
*Preparation time 15 minutes*
*Cooking time 20 minutes*

**8oz boneless, skinless chicken breast, thinly sliced**

**½ teaspoon salt**

**½ teaspoon sugar**

**1 tablespoon potato starch**

**3 tablespoons water**

**1 tablespoon vegetable oil**

**1 tablespoon fermented black beans**

**1 garlic clove, minced**

**1 medium onion, cut into ½-inch dice**

**2 green peppers, cut into ½-inch dice**

**½ cup chicken stock** *(see page 12)*

**1 teaspoon potato starch mixture**
*(see page 8)*

**\*Lisa's tips**

*To preserve the black beans add*
*1 tablespoon of vegetable oil to the jar*
*so they don't dry out.*

I've taught this dish to hundreds of novice cooks at the Sweet Mandarin Cooking School, and this is a consistent favorite. The addition of fermented black beans brings a depth of flavor to the dish that a jar of black bean sauce could never replicate. The two-step process of "velveting" the chicken in a simple marinade then blanching it before adding it to the dish ensures the chicken stays tender and the peppers retain a crunch.

METHOD

Put the chicken in a bowl, add the salt, sugar, potato starch, and water, and set aside to marinate for 10 minutes (or longer if time permits).

Fill a wok with boiling water and bring to a boil. Add the marinated chicken, turn down the heat to a gentle simmer, and poach the chicken for 10 minutes or until cooked through. Drain in a colander and run the chicken under cold water to halt the cooking process; set aside. Carefully pour out the water from the wok and dry the pan.

Put the wok over medium heat and add the oil. Add the black beans and cook for 1 minute, stirring, to release their aroma into the oil. Next add the garlic, onion, peppers, and cooked chicken and stir-fry for 5 minutes.

Pour in the chicken stock, bring to a boil, and check for seasoning; you might need a little extra salt or sugar. Once the stock is bubbling, add the potato starch mixture and stir vigorously until the sauce thickens.

# LEMON CHICKEN DELUXE
## 檸檬雞

*Gluten free*

*Dairy free*

*Serves 2*

*Preparation time 15 minutes*

*Cooking time 15 minutes*

**2 boneless chicken breasts**

**1 teaspoon salt**

**1 teaspoon sugar**

**5 tablespoons potato starch, plus**
    **extra for coating**

**2 tablespoons water**

**vegetable oil, for deep-frying**

**1 egg, beaten**

*For the lemon sauce*

**2 tablespoons lemon juice**

**¼ cup water**

**3 tablespoons sugar**

**2 strips of lemon zest, removed with**
    **a vegetable peeler**

**1 teaspoon potato starch mixture**
    *(see page 8)*

*To garnish*

**sprig of parsley**

**2 lemon slices**

**\*Lisa's tips**

*The lemon sauce can be made sweeter by using honey. Ensure only the rind is used for the lemon zest since the white of the lemon can be bitter.*

Lemon Chicken Deluxe was born from a clash of culinary cultures when Hong Kong became a British colony under the 1842 Treaty of Nanking. This dish reflected the temper of the times—fresh, tart, and daring. Typical Chinese food rarely paired the sourness of lemons with chicken, but during this period Hong Kong became an increasingly popular destination for Western travelers, who influenced tastes and loved sweet and sour.

British men were sent out to Hong Kong for plum jobs in Hong Kong's institutions. Many were talented and ambitious men with connections to royalty and politics. Many brought their families to enjoy the good weather and carefree lifestyle, treating it as an extended holiday. Hong Kong was exciting, a new world full of life and bizarre Chinese ways of living. This dish reflected the mood perfectly.

METHOD

First prepare the chicken. Butterfly each breast to speed up the cooking process: put the chicken breast on a clean work surface. Hold a long, sharp knife along the long side of the chicken. Using a sawing motion, slice through the breast almost to the end. Fold out the chicken, press to flatten and put in a bowl. Season with the salt and sugar and stir in the potato starch and water. Set aside to marinate for 10 minutes.

Meanwhile, fill a wok with approx. ½ cup oil and preheat over medium heat to 350°F. Test the temperature of the oil with a bamboo chopstick (see page 35).

Remove the pieces of chicken from the marinade and dip first into the beaten egg and then into the potato starch to create a light batter. Lower the battered chicken into the hot oil and deep-fry for 5 minutes until cooked through. Remove with a slotted spoon and drain on paper towels. Transfer the chicken to a clean chopping board and slice into ½ x 2-inch pieces. Arrange on a serving plate.

To make the lemon sauce, heat a wok and add all the ingredients, except the potato starch mixture. Bring to a boil and then add the potato starch mixture, stirring vigorously until the sauce thickens.

To serve, spoon the lemony sauce over the hot, crispy chicken and garnish with parsley and the lemon slices.

# SZECHUAN DRIED SPICED CHICKEN
## 四川辣子雞

🌾 Gluten free

❤ Dairy free

◖ Egg free

Serves 2

Preparation time 10 minutes

Cooking time 20 minutes

**6oz boneless, skinless chicken breasts, cut into even slices**

**1½ teaspoons salt**

**1½ teaspoons sugar**

**1 tablespoon potato starch**

**3 tablespoons water**

**2 tablespoons vegetable oil**

**3 garlic cloves, sliced**

**1 medium onion, finely sliced**

**2 scallions, finely sliced**

**12 dried red chiles (or more if you want extra heat)**

**1 tablespoon Szechuan peppercorns**

**3 tablespoons Shaoxing rice wine**

**\*Lisa's tips**

*Don't stand over the wok when you add the chiles or the fumes will sting your eyes.*

The Szechuan province of China is known as the province of abundance. Indeed, chiles from this region make the top quartile of the Scoville rating, the scale named after American chemist Wilbur Scoville who developed the test in 1912 as a measure of the "hotness" of a chile pepper (or anything derived from chile peppers, such as hot sauce). When I visited the province I remember seeing a scarlet sea of dried chiles as long as a football field—actually a market with numerous vendors of dried chiles.

This is one addictive dish, literally. Szechuans are used to eating chiles with everything and if they don't eat enough of them they get withdrawal symptoms! Chiles contain a chemical called capsaicin, which gives the heat, acts as a relaxant, and provides many health benefits, including lowering blood pressure, boosting circulation, and reducing inflammation. I remember the first time I tried this dish. There was no doubt it was spicy, but it was also so tasty I couldn't stop eating it, and before long the whole plate had been eaten by ME!—I knew right away that it would be a winner when served at Sweet Mandarin.

METHOD

Combine the chicken in a bowl with ½ teaspoon of salt, ½ teaspoon of sugar, the potato starch, and water, and set aside to marinate for 10 minutes.

Add 1 tablespoon of oil to a hot wok and stir-fry the chicken for 10 minutes over high heat until cooked through. Remove the chicken from the wok and set aside on a plate. Don't rinse the wok because you want to retain the flavors from the chicken.

Return the wok to high heat and put in 1 tablespoon of oil. Add the garlic, onion, and scallions and stir-fry for 4 minutes until the onions have softened and browned slightly. Reduce the heat and quickly stir in the dried red chiles.

Return the cooked chicken to the wok along with the Szechuan peppercorns. Season with 1 teaspoon each of salt and sugar. Pour in the Shaoxing wine and cook for 3 minutes, stirring vigorously to keep the ingredients moving so they don't stick or burn. Serve with an ice-cold Chinese beer.

# DAD'S CHICKEN-FRIED RICE
## 雞柳炒飯

🌾 *Use tamari rather than soy sauce.*

♥ *Dairy free*

*Serves 2*

*Preparation time 5 minutes*

*Cooking time 10 minutes*

**2 tablespoons vegetable oil**

**1 egg, beaten**

**1 cup cooled boiled rice**

**1½ cups sliced cooked chicken**

**¼ cup peas or corn**

**1 teaspoon salt**

**1 drop of light soy sauce**

**\*Lisa's tips**

*Cooked rice should be stored in the fridge for no longer than 2 days.*

This is our dad's favorite dish. We make it for him on Father's Day, but the rest of the year he makes it for himself! Recently, it has also become a big hit with our nephew Sam. I hope your family will love it, too.

METHOD

Add 1 tablespoon of oil to a preheated wok, pour in the beaten egg, and scramble quickly with a fork until set. Add the rice, reduce the heat to low, and pat out the grains to separate them. Once the rice has separated, scoop it onto a plate and set aside.

Clean the wok, preheat it over high heat and add the remaining oil. Add the cooked chicken slices and peas or corn, and stir-fry for 5 minutes. Return the cooked egg-fried rice to the wok, toss well, and cook for another 5 minutes. Season with salt and a splash of light soy sauce.

# CHINESE CHICKEN SALAD *(Grandma's first ever salad)*
# 中式雞柳沙律

*Gluten free*

*Dairy free*

*Egg free*

*Serves 2*

*Preparation time 5 minutes*

*Cooking time 10 minutes*

**¾ cup edamame beans**

**¾ cup green beans, cut into**
**1-inch lengths**

**⅓ cucumber, cut in half lengthwise**
**and sliced into half-moon shapes**

**8oz cherry tomatoes, halved**

**8oz salad leaves, such as lettuce,**
**arugula, or mixed greens,**
**washed and dried**

**6 tablespoons sweet chile sauce**
*(see page 14)*

**1½ cups cooked chicken breast, sliced**

**lime wedges, to garnish**

**\*Lisa's tips**

*Sweet Mandarin Sweet Chile sauce is a*
*natural aphrodisiac because of the fresh*
*chiles used.*

When our grandmother arrived at the docks of Liverpool in the 1950s, she was astonished to see a white woman scrubbing the portside. Lily had served only British families and had never seen them do manual jobs. World War II had ended and Britain was changing. Women now worked in what were previously classed as men's jobs. Britain celebrated victory with patriotic propaganda, yet Britain was an exhausted nation, bankrupt and broken. Millions of people were on the move looking for families and homes; there was a shortage of labor, and foreigners were welcome, initially.

Our grandmother first learned about salad at these docks. Chinese cuisine rarely serves dishes cold, but a shortage of food meant people had to be creative. On that particular day, as the ship docked, there was an abundance of lettuces and, noticing Lily's smile, the grocer handed her a battered and bruised one, commenting that her smile had brightened up his day. On the ship there were also chicken carcasses, so Lily scraped the meat from the bones to create a simple dish that surprised even her.

I have added to her basic recipe to take into account the abundance of vegetables we are now fortunate enough to have available. This is a great dish for using up leftover roast chicken to create a quick light lunch or dinner. Our sweet chile sauce is versatile and can be used as a cold dressing as well as reheated and served as a hot sauce.

METHOD

Blanch the edamame beans and green beans for 5 minutes in boiling water; drain and refresh under cold running water.

Combine all the salad ingredients in a mixing bowl, add 3 tablespoons of sweet chile sauce, and toss well to combine.

Scoop the dressed salad onto a plate, arrange the cooked chicken slices on top, and drizzle on another 3 tablespoons of the sweet chile sauce. Garnish with lime wedges.

# FIRECRACKER CHICKEN
# 宮保雞丁

**〇** *Omit the chile bean paste and use fresh red chiles instead.*

**♥** *Dairy free*

**〇** *Egg free*

*Serves 2*

*Preparation time 15 minutes*

*Cooking time 20 minutes*

**8oz boneless, skinless chicken breasts, cut into 1-inch slices**

**1½ teaspoons salt**

**2 teaspoons sugar**

**1 tablespoon potato starch or cornstarch**

**4 teaspoons water**

**1 tablespoon vegetable oil**

**1-inch piece of fresh ginger, peeled and finely sliced**

**1 medium onion, diced into ½-inch cubes**

**1 carrot, peeled and sliced into rounds**

**1 x 6oz can of sliced bamboo shoots**

**1 heaping teaspoon chile bean paste**

**⅔ cup chicken stock** *(see page 12)*

**⅔ cup sweet and sour sauce** *(see page 14)*

**2 teaspoons potato starch mixture** *(see page 8)*

**a handful of toasted cashew nuts or unsalted peanuts**

This dish combines the yin and yang of Chinese cooking with its warming and cooling elements. The ginger and chile bean paste create a warming, seductive sauce while the bamboo shoots and chicken cool the dish down. This recipe is not fiendishly hot, but it does have a gentle kick to awaken your taste buds—you'll certainly feel some heat on the back of the palate after you've tasted a bite. Spice up your evening with this little firecracker of a dish.

METHOD

Put the chicken in a bowl and mix in 1 teaspoon of salt, 1 teaspoon of sugar, the potato starch (or cornstarch), and water. Cover the bowl with plastic wrap and set aside to marinate for at least 10 minutes.

Fill a medium saucepan with water and bring to a boil. Add the chicken pieces, reduce the heat to a gentle simmer, and poach for 5–7 minutes until cooked through. Drain through a colander and run under cold water to stop the cooking process. Drain and set aside on a plate.

Heat a wok over high heat, add the oil, and heat until starting to smoke. Throw in the ginger slices and stir-fry for 1 minute to infuse the oil. Add the onion, carrot, and bamboo shoots and stir-fry briefly. Put in the cooked chicken and stir-fry for 5 minutes. Stir in the chile bean paste and cook for 2 minutes to release the aroma of the chiles.

Pour in the chicken stock, add the sweet and sour sauce, and season with ½ teaspoon of salt and 1 teaspoon of sugar.

Bring the sauce to a boil then add the potato starch mixture, stirring vigorously until it thickens. Finally, add the roasted cashew nuts or peanuts, and toss lightly to coat them in the sauce.

# MABEL'S CLAY POT CHICKEN
# 滑雞煲

*Use tamari rather than oyster sauce and soy sauce.*

*Dairy free*

*Egg free*

Serves 2

Preparation time 10 minutes

Cooking time 30 minutes

**2 tablespoons vegetable oil**

**4 garlic cloves, sliced**

**1-inch piece of fresh ginger, peeled and sliced**

**1 medium onion, finely sliced**

**1 scallion, finely sliced**

**½ Chinese sausage (lap cheong), sliced**

**8oz boneless, skinless chicken breasts, cut into bite-sized pieces**

**1⅓ cups shredded Napa cabbage**

**¼ cup water**

**½ teaspoon salt**

**½ tablespoon sugar**

**3 tablespoons oyster sauce**

**1 tablespoon sesame oil**

**1 tablespoon dark soy sauce**

**2 tablespoons Shaoxing rice wine**

**2 tablespoons potato starch mixture**
*(see page 8)*

**2 blanched bok choy leaves, to garnish**

\*Lisa's tips

*Lap cheong is similar to salami, very intense in flavor and quite sweet. Only a few slices are needed per serving.*

Our mother, Mabel, remarked that she lost her childhood innocence when she arrived in England in 1959. Her mother, Lily, had left her and her brother Arthur in Hong Kong for three years while Lily carved out her business in the UK. When Lily brought Mabel, aged 9, and Arthur, aged 12, to England, Mabel hated the country immediately, and she hated Lily for bringing her there. Mabel missed the sunshine, her friends, the food, and most of all her grandmother, who had become like a surrogate mother.

Mabel arrived on a dark winter afternoon and remembers shivering in the street while Lily unloaded the bags. Residents came out of their houses and, standing on the doorsteps with their arms folded, they tutted and whispered to one another: "First one Chinese, now two more. It's a bloody infestation! What is the world coming to? Did we fight a war for this?" My mother had no experience of racism and, young as she was, she understood the sentiment as surely as if her new neighbors had punched her in the face. However, it was through this dish that the animosity between mother and daughter melted away. As the chicken was stir-fried and the rice wine was added, my mother was instantly transported back to Hong Kong, and she picked up her chopsticks with relish. This was her comfort food.

We cooked this dish for Gordon Ramsay on the *F Word* and it won us the title of Best Local Chinese Restaurant in the UK. We dedicated the award to our mother.

METHOD

Heat a wok over high heat and add the oil. Fry the garlic, ginger, onion, scallion, and Chinese sausage for 2 minutes over high heat. Add the chicken and Napa cabbage and stir-fry for 5–7 minutes. Add the water, salt, sugar, oyster sauce, sesame oil, dark soy sauce, and Shaoxing wine. Bring the sauce to a boil then add the potato starch mixture, stirring vigorously to thicken.

Pour into a clay pot or large, heavy-bottomed casserole, cover with the lid, and cook over low heat for 15 minutes to allow the sauce to infuse the chicken. Garnish with two blanched bok choy leaves.

# CANTONESE-STYLE ROAST CHICKEN
# 港式烤雞

*Use tamari rather than soy sauce.*

*Dairy free*

*Egg free*

*Serves 4*

*Preparation time 10 hours*

*Cooking time 1½ hours*

**3 lb whole chicken**

**2 whole garlic heads**

**1-inch piece of fresh ginger**
    **(kept whole)**

*For the marinade*

**5 tablespoons dark soy sauce**

**5 tablespoons honey**

**5 teaspoons Shaoxing rice wine**

**5 teaspoons sesame oil**

**1 teaspoon salt**

**1 teaspoon white pepper**

**\*Lisa's tips**

*Ensure the chicken is as dry as possible
before putting it in the oven so the skin
crisps up nicely.*

Cantonese-style roast chicken quite literally blew traditional roast chicken out of the water—well, that is according to our grandmother. Back in the 1950s, when she was working as a maid and cook in Hong Kong, Lily had to cook all the meals for the family on a baked-mud stove fired with charcoal—and this is what she used to prepare for Sunday lunch. It is a classic Cantonese dish with a deeper flavor than ordinary roast chicken because it absorbs all the Chinese flavors during the overnight marinating.

METHOD

Wash the chicken under cold running water and pat dry on paper towels inside and out. Stuff the chicken cavity with the whole garlic heads and ginger.

Pour the ingredients for the marinade into a large plastic ziplock bag and mix well. Put in the chicken, basting well, seal, and transfer to the fridge to marinate overnight.

Preheat the oven to 425°F. Meanwhile, take the chicken out of the plastic bag, put it on a rack inside a roasting pan, and air-dry for 30 minutes. This air-drying process is important because it will help the skin to crisp up.

Put the chicken in the hot oven and roast for 1¼ hours. Remove from the oven and set aside to rest for 15 minutes before carving.

Generations of Chinese families have always cooked with pork. This tradition is linked to rearing pigs on their premises where the pigs became an integral part of family life. Today eating pork still represents strength, wealth, and abundant blessing. Beef is also used in Chinese dishes but ultimately pork is the preferred protein.

The combination of texture, aroma, and flavor makes these meat recipes special and unique. The magic of the dish comes from the cooking technique; steaming, braising, roasting, stir-frying, and pan-frying are all used to make the most of a fabulous piece of meat.

This chapter features meals that, once tasted, will stay with you as a lingering, amazingly satisfying memory for life. When I first tried Chairman Mao's Red Cooked Pork, I remember squealing in delight at the inky-red morsels of melt-in-your-mouth pork and savoring the flavors of China. Then there are recipes such as the Asian-style Burger, which pays homage to *Iron Chef*—one of the hardest cooking competitions I have ever competed in, but one that took my culinary skills to another level. A melange of mantou buns and burgers sat there like little soldiers ready to fight against the *Iron Chef* and the beet relish was a great complement to the rich, meaty burger.

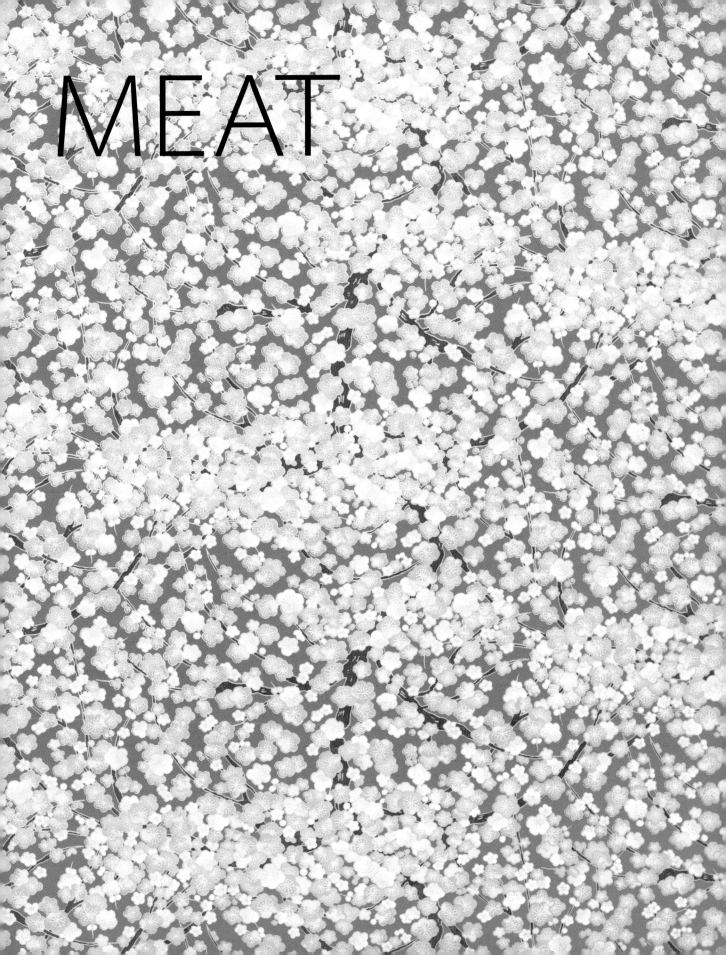

# MEAT

# SWEET MANDARIN BARBECUE RIBS
## 燒排骨

*Gluten free*

*Dairy free*

*Egg free*

*Serves 2*

*Preparation time 10 minutes*

*Cooking time 1½ hours*

**1 lb rack of baby back ribs**

**1¼ cups Barbecue sauce** *(see page 15)*

**\*Lisa's tips**

*This is such a simple dish with no overnight marinating! Ask your butcher to remove the tough, translucent membrane from the back of the rack to make the ribs extra tender.*

In many ways, the late 1950s marked a watershed for the UK and for pork ribs. Previously pork ribs had rarely been used as an ingredient, with people preferring to serve roast beef during the UK's heyday, but after two World Wars, people were forced to choose a cheaper option. The only problem was that pork didn't have the depth of flavor of beef and many people were put off because it was fatty. This is where our grandmother stepped in. In time, her wonderfully aromatic marinated and barbecued pork ribs became more popular than any beef dish on the menu.

This is a really easy recipe for ribs, and there is no overnight marinade needed. Cooking the ribs in a low oven makes the meat meltingly tender and prevents the sauce from burning.

METHOD

Preheat the oven to 400°F.

Wash the ribs in the sink. Cover a roasting pan with foil and lay the ribs on top. Pour three-quarters of the barbecue sauce over the ribs, and baste the meat on both sides.

Reduce the oven temperature to 300°F and transfer the ribs to the oven to slow-cook for 1 hour.

After an hour, increase the temperature to 400°F and continue to cook for 25 minutes more until the sauce bubbles and caramelizes.

Remove the ribs from the oven and set aside to rest before carving. Serve with a salad and the rest of the barbecue sauce.

# BRAISED PORK BELLY AND BOK CHOY
紅燒火腩

🌾 *Use tamari rather than soy sauce.*

💧 *Dairy free*

⭕ *Egg free*

*Serves 2*

*Preparation time 15 minutes*

*Cooking time 15 minutes*

8oz boneless white fish, cut into
    1-inch pieces

5oz tofu

4 tablespoons vegetable oil

1-inch piece of fresh ginger,
    peeled and sliced

1 cinnamon stick

8oz piece of cooked pork belly
    *(see page 88),* cut into
    ¼ x 1-inch strips

1 cup chicken stock *(see page 12)*

5–6 dried Chinese mushrooms,
    soaked in boiling water for
    15 minutes then halved

3 bok choy leaves, cut into
    bite-sized pieces

½ teaspoon salt, plus extra for
    seasoning the fish

½ teaspoon sugar

1 teaspoon dark soy sauce

1 teaspoon sesame oil

1 tablespoon Shaoxing rice wine

2 tablespoons potato starch mixture
    *(see page 8)*

**\*Lisa's tips**

*You can also use raw pork belly for this—
just make sure you cook it thoroughly for
10 minutes.*

I always enjoyed family dinners when I was growing up, not only for the good, hearty food but also for the stories and running commentaries about the business and day-to-day life. This dish has always been popular in the Tse household and each person has their own favorite part—Mom loves the bok choy, Dad loves the fish, and I love the pork belly! I hope it's a hit with your family, too.

METHOD

Season the fish with a pinch of salt. Prepare the tofu by cutting it into long blocks 1 inch wide.

Preheat the wok over medium heat, add the oil, and fry the tofu for 3–4 minutes until crisp. Remove from the wok and set aside.

Return the wok to high heat, add the ginger and cinnamon stick, and stir-fry for 1 minute to release their fragrance into the oil. Put in the strips of cooked pork belly and stir-fry for 4 minutes. Pour in the chicken stock, add the mushrooms, bok choy, and fish pieces, and cook for another 5 minutes until the chicken stock is bubbling and the fish is cooked through. Season with salt, sugar, soy sauce, sesame oil, and Shaoxing wine.

Bring to a boil and add the potato starch mixture, stirring vigorously until the sauce thickens. Finally add the cooked tofu pieces, and toss to coat them in the sauce. Serve with jasmine rice.

# CRISPY PORK BELLY
# 脆皮燒肉

*Serves 2*

*Preparation time 10 hours*

*Cooking time 1 hour*

**2 teaspoons salt**

**2 teaspoons sugar**

**½ teaspoon five spice powder**

**1½ lbs pork belly**

**½ tablespoon Shaoxing rice wine**

**1 teaspoon salt, to taste**

**\*Lisa's tips**

*Make sure you keep the skin as dry as possible before the pork goes into the oven. This will ensure you get really good crackling.*

*Any leftovers can be used in the Braised Pork Belly and Bok choy recipe on page 86.*

When I asked my closest friends, family, customers, and students what their favorite dish was, my brother Jim said he was a big fan of crispy pork belly. He said he even loves eating it cold and always ends up eating too much!

This is the recipe for pork belly our grandmother used to make when we were small. Lily was especially proud of the fact that even though belly is a cheap cut of meat, her cooking method transformed it into food fit for a king. She was certainly right. I can still remember our whoops of delight and utter satisfaction as we bit into the crispy crackling.

METHOD

Combine the salt, sugar, and five spice powder in a bowl and set aside. Using a sharp knife, scrape away any impurities and hair from the rind of the pork. Rinse thoroughly.

Bring 6 cups of water to a boil in a wok, put in the pork belly, and simmer gently for 15 minutes to soften the skin. Drain well and pat dry on paper towels; the rind, in particular, needs to be as dry as possible.

Using a sharp knife, poke as many holes in the rind as possible, but try not to pierce into the meat. The holes release the fat as it cooks, helping the rind to crisp up.

Rub the seasonings and Shaoxing wine over the flesh side of the meat; do not get any of the seasoning on the rind. Put the pork on a sheet of foil, flesh-side down, and wrap up the sides tightly, keeping the rind uncovered. Transfer the pork to the fridge overnight, during which time the seasoning will penetrate the flesh and the skin will dry out completely.

Preheat the oven to 425°F.

Remove the pork from fridge and take off the foil. Put the pork, skin-side up, on a rack set inside a roasting pan. Rub the salt into the rind to season it.

Transfer the pork to the hot oven for 15 minutes, and then reduce the temperature to 400°F and continue to cook for another 45 minutes.

To serve, cut the pork into slices and accompany with rice.

# CHAR SIU ROAST PORK
## 蜜汁叉燒

*Use tamari rather than soy sauce and hoisin sauce.*

*Dairy free*

*Egg free*

*Serves 2*

*Preparation and marinade time 10 hours*

*Cooking time 1 hour*

**1 lb pork tenderloin**

**2 garlic cloves, minced**

**2 tablespoons vegetable oil**

*For the char siu sauce*

**2 tablespoons brown sugar**

**2 tablespoons honey**

**2 tablespoons hoisin sauce**

**2 tablespoons dark soy sauce**

**2 tablespoons Shaoxing rice wine**

**2 dashes of ground white pepper**

**½ teaspoon paprika**

**½ teaspoon five spice powder**

**2 teaspoons sesame oil**

**\*Lisa's tips**

*The secret to this delicious slab of meat is the overnight marinating, which softens the pork and infuses it with sweet aromatics. Any leftovers can be used for stir-fries or in a fried rice or noodle dish such as Singapore Vermicelli (page 150).*

Our grandfather Kwok Chan was like a cat with nine lives. He flirted with danger and had probably exhausted eight lives already when, on a cold winter's day, he fell into the icy waters off Hong Kong after a frantic police chase. A cold mist enveloped his body and the bitter wind penetrated his light clothing, but Chan didn't despair. Recounting his adventures to his family afterward, our grandfather admitted that his last meal had been char siu: "If I had died, I would have died a happy man as there is nothing more satisfying than char siu."

METHOD

Combine all the ingredients for the char siu sauce in a saucepan. Heat over high heat until bubbling and then remove from the heat and set aside to cool.

Put the pork in a large plastic ziplock bag with the minced garlic and vegetable oil. Pour in the cold char siu sauce and mix thoroughly to ensure the pork is evenly coated. Set aside to marinate in the fridge overnight.

Preheat the oven to 425°F.

Remove the pork from the fridge and transfer it to a roasting pan. Brush the marinade over the pork and roast in the oven for 30 minutes. Remove the pork from the oven and baste well before returning it to the oven for another 20–30 minutes.

To serve, cut the pork into slices and serve with jasmine rice.

# SPICY DOUBLE-COOKED PORK WITH LEEKS
# 回鍋肉

🌾 *Omit the chile bean paste and yellow bean paste and use 2 teaspoons of minced garlic instead.*

♥ *Dairy free*

○ *Egg free*

*Serves 2*

*Preparation time 30 minutes*

*Cooking time 30 minutes*

**10oz pork belly, rind removed, but retain the fat for added flavor**

**2 tablespoons vegetable oil**

**1-inch piece of fresh ginger, peeled and sliced**

**1 garlic clove, sliced**

**1 medium onion, finely sliced**

**1 leek, finely sliced**

**2 teaspoons chile bean paste**

**2 teaspoons yellow bean paste**

**½ teaspoon dark soy sauce**

**1 teaspoon sugar**

**½ cup chicken stock** *(see page 12)*

**\*Lisa's tips**

*Chile bean paste takes over 40 days to make, since the beans need to ferment. Therefore, we recommend buying a jar of ready-made paste. It's very powerful stuff so you only need a small amount. Once opened, store in the fridge and use within 4 weeks.*

When we returned to the village where our grandmother grew up, the streets were deadly quiet. There were no cars, motorcycles, or bicycles. No bells, no horns, no animals. Only the delighted shrieks of awestruck children receiving sweets from our grandmother resonated. In the fields behind the house, there was a shout from a martial arts competition. We observed the deep, introspective silence of the old barber, sitting in his brown silk pajamas on a plastic stool, waiting for someone to come in for a shave. And elsewhere there was the soft whirring of an old sewing machine, pedalled by the dressmaker in his shop. To our surprise, this was all that remained of the village where our grandmother grew up.

It was a memorable visit for our grandmother, returning to her village after 60 years' absence, but one of the remarkable memories for me was the food we enjoyed that day, which was cooked for us by an old relative from another era. This is one of the truly inspirational dishes he prepared for us.

METHOD

Half-fill a wok with water and bring to a boil. Drop in the pork belly and simmer for about 20 minutes, or until cooked through. Drain the pork and set aside on a plate to cool. Transfer the pork to the fridge for 15 minutes, uncovered, to firm up.

Remove the pork belly from the fridge and slice into thin strips. Add the oil to a hot wok and stir-fry the pork for 5 minutes until slightly crisp. Add the ginger, garlic, onion, and leek, and stir-fry briefly to combine. Stir in the chile bean and yellow bean pastes, the soy sauce, sugar, and chicken stock, and cook for another 5 minutes until the sauce is bubbling.

# PEKING PORK CHOPS
## 北京豬扒

*Use tamari rather than soy sauce.*

*Dairy free*

*Egg free*

*Serves 2*

*Preparation time 10 minutes*

*Cooking time 20 minutes*

**2 x 5oz boneless pork loin chops**

**pinch of salt**

**2 tablespoons vegetable oil**

**½ teaspoon minced garlic**

**1 medium onion, finely sliced**

**1 green pepper, finely sliced**

*For the Peking sauce*

**2 tablespoons ketchup**

**1 tablespoon yellow bean paste**

**1 tablespoon plum sauce**

**1 tablespoon steak sauce**

**1 tablespoon Worcestershire sauce**

**1 tablespoon sugar**

**½ teaspoon salt**

*For the garnish*

**1 tablespoon sesame seeds**

*** Lisa's tips**

*Bring the pork chops to room temperature
before cooking. To make them extra juicy,
marinate them with a splash of apple juice
for 15 minutes in the fridge before cooking.*

This dish is often enjoyed for Chinese New Year. The pig symbolizes abundance, prosperity, and a plump year ahead; the glaze is sweet to represent a sweet new year and the unity of family and friends; while the red color is appealing to the eye and lucky in Chinese culture because red symbolizes luck and celebration.

METHOD

Rub the pork chops all over with a pinch of salt. Add 1 tablespoon of oil to a hot wok and pan-fry the pork chops over medium heat for 5 minutes on each side or until cooked through. Remove the pork chops from the wok and set aside on a plate

Clean the wok and put it back over high heat. Add the remaining tablespoon of oil and stir-fry the garlic, onion, and pepper for 2–3 minutes over medium heat. Add all the ingredients for the Peking sauce and bring to a boil.

Return the cooked pork to the wok, spoon over some of the bubbling sauce and simmer for 5 minutes. Sprinkle with the sesame seeds and serve.

# STEAMED PORK SPARE RIBS WITH BLACK BEANS

# 豉汁蒸排骨

*Gluten free*

*Dairy free*

*Egg free*

*Serves 2*

*Preparation time 20 minutes*

*Cooking time 20 minutes*

**10oz pork spare ribs, cut into 2-inch lengths**

**2 garlic cloves, finely chopped**

**2 tablespoons fermented black beans**

**1 teaspoon salt**

**1 teaspoon sugar**

**3 scallions, finely sliced**

**\*Lisa's tips**

*Ask your butcher to cut the ribs into 2-inch lengths for you.*

Our great-grandmother used to rear pigs on a small piece of land adjacent to a lake. Usually Tai Po and her husband would catch and slaughter the pigs together, but one year her husband was ill and so she was forced to do the job herself. Wrestling a pig singlehandedly is hard work, and soon Tai Po ended up being pushed into the lake by the pig's brethren, who had come to the rescue. Although she was only in the water for a few minutes, it was long enough for her wet winter clothes to freeze her body stiff, and she managed to swallow gallons of water. Thankfully, a neighboring farmer was alerted by her spluttered cries for help and managed to drag her, muddied but alive, onto land. Not wanting the pig to have the last laugh, she vowed that the pig should be caught, butchered, and cooked that day so that her efforts would not have been in vain. The family have a little chuckle every time we make this dish. My mother jokes that she cut the spare ribs into 2-inch pieces as sweet revenge for that dramatic experience in the lake (although actually it accelerates the cooking time and ensures the flavors permeate all parts of the dish). Incidentally, this dish is one of the top ten dim sum.

METHOD

First marinate the ribs. Put them in a shallow heatproof bowl and mix with the garlic, fermented black beans, salt, and sugar. Cover with foil and set aside to marinate in the fridge for 20 minutes.

Remove the foil and put the bowl of ribs inside a preheated steamer and steam for 15 minutes or until the juices run clear. Check the water level after 10 minutes and top up if necessary with more water. If you don't have a steamer, you can use a wok instead (see page 127).

Remove the lid of the steamer, sprinkle on the scallions and steam for another 5 minutes.

To serve, carefully remove the bowl of ribs from the steamer and serve them with jasmine rice.

# CHAIRMAN MAO'S RED COOKED PORK
# 毛主席紅燒肉

*Serves 2*

*Preparation time 10 minutes*

*Cooking time 2 hours*

**14oz boneless pork belly, cut into**
  **2-inch cubes**

**3 tablespoons vegetable oil**

*For the sauce*

**½ cup dark soy sauce**

**2 tablespoons light soy sauce**

**2 tablespoons hoisin sauce**

**¼ cup brown sugar**

**2-inch piece of fresh ginger**
  **(kept whole)**

**2 star anise**

**2-inch piece of cassia bark**

**2 garlic cloves, minced**

**¾ cup daikon or turnip, peeled and**
  **cut into 2-inch cubes**

*∗**Lisa's tips***
*You can also add carrots to the dish,*
*which will give it extra sweetness.*
*If you have any leftovers, this dish is even*
*more delicious reheated the next day.*

This was Chairman Mao's favorite dish and it is not surprising. The dark red, caramelized sauce penetrates deep into the pork during the slow-cooking process, making it sweet and succulent and meltingly tender.

One of the key ingredients in this dish is soy sauce. There are two kinds of soy sauce, dark and light, with the light soy sauce tasting considerably saltier than the dark. In this dish, we include dark soy sauce for color and light soy sauce for flavor.

METHOD

Fill a saucepan with $1^2/_3$ cups water and bring to a boil. Add the pork and simmer for 15 minutes until cooked through. Remove the pork with a slotted spoon and drain on paper towels; set aside. Skim the scum from the cooking liquid and measure out ¾ cup into a measuring cup; discard the rest.

Heat a second deep saucepan until hot and add the vegetable oil. Put in the cooked pieces of pork and brown well on all sides for about 5 minutes. Pour in the reserved cooking liquid and add the ingredients for the sauce. Bring to a boil, cover the pan with a lid, and simmer gently for 1 hour. Add the chopped daikon or turnip and continue to cook for another 30 minutes.

# MR. WOODMAN'S BEEF, ONIONS, AND BROCCOLI
## 西蘭花炒牛柳

🌾 *Omit the oyster sauce.*

♥ *Dairy free*

◐ *Egg free*

*Serves 2*

*Preparation time 15 minutes*

*Cooking time 20 minutes*

**5 tablespoons vegetable oil**

**10oz beef sirloin, thinly sliced**

**1 garlic clove, finely sliced**

**1 medium broccoli, florets separated**

**1 medium onion, finely sliced**

**¼ cup chicken stock** *(see page 12)*
  **or beef stock**

*For the sauce*

**1 tablespoon oyster sauce**

**1 teaspoon Shaoxing rice wine**

**1 teaspoon sesame oil**

**½ teaspoon salt**

**½ teaspoon sugar**

**2 tablespoons potato starch mixture**

  *(see page 8)*

**\*Lisa's tips**

*Cut the vegetables and the beef into similar-sized pieces to ensure they cook evenly.*
*To make the meat extra tender, we sear the sliced meat in vegetable oil first, which locks in the juices.*

The last family our grandmother worked for in Hong Kong were the Woodmans, who loved her like their own daughter. It was for Mr. Woodman, who was responsible for the entire electricity supply to Hong Kong, that she developed this recipe. It is a quick and easy dish to cook, and I hope your family will love it, too. The two-step cooking process ensures the beef is perfectly cooked while the broccoli stays crisp.

METHOD

This first step is a restaurant secret to ensure the beef remains soft and juicy. Add the oil to a hot wok, drop in the slices of beef, and stir-fry over high heat for 5 minutes or until cooked to your liking. Remove with a slotted spoon and set aside on a plate. Drain off the oil, but don't wash the wok.

Return the wok to low heat—it should still be lightly coated with oil—and stir-fry the garlic, broccoli, and onion for 4 minutes. Add the slices of cooked beef, pour in the stock, and bring to a boil. Simmer for 5 minutes.

Add all the ingredients for the sauce, except the potato starch mixture, and bring to a boil. Once the sauce is bubbling, add the potato starch mixture and stir vigorously to thicken the dish. Serve hot with boiled rice.

# KWOK CHAN'S BRAISED BEEF BRISKET CASSEROLE
## 蘿蔔炆牛腩

*Use tamari rather than soy sauce.*

*Dairy free*

*Egg free*

*Preparation time 10 minutes*

*Cooking time 2¼ hours*

**10oz beef brisket, cut into 2-inch cubes**

**3 tablespoons vegetable oil**

**4 tablespoons Shaoxing rice wine**

**1½-inch piece of fresh ginger (kept whole)**

**4 garlic cloves, sliced**

**4 star anise**

**1 tablespoon five spice powder**

**1 tablespoon dark soy sauce**

**1 medium daikon, cut into 2-inch cubes**

**1 medium onion, cut into 1-inch cubes**

**\*Lisa's tips**

*A slow cooker is ideal for this recipe as it needs time to slowly tenderize the beef brisket.*

Our grandfather was named Kwok Chan. He was born in 1914 and started life in Guangzhou, where his family owned a restaurant. The specialty at the family restaurant was braised beef brisket with daikon. It was a popular dish, created over 200 years ago during the Qing Dynasty, and apparently people traveled from all over China to sample it. According to our grandmother, Kwok Chan was unruly, associated with Triad members, and full of vices. However, she couldn't fault his braised beef brisket: "That's probably why I stayed with him—and the kids."

METHOD

Fill a medium saucepan with water and bring to a boil. Add the beef and simmer for 15 minutes; drain, discarding the cooking liquid.

Heat a heavy-bottomed saucepan over high heat and add the oil. Put in the drained beef, reduce the heat to medium, and brown on all sides for about 15 minutes. Remove the meat from the pan and set aside on a plate.

Return the pan to the heat, add the Shaoxing wine, and deglaze the pan by loosening any meaty pieces stuck to the bottom with a wooden spoon. Put in the ginger, garlic, star anise, five spice powder, and soy sauce, and cook for 5 minutes, stirring. Return the beef to the pan and pour in enough cold water to cover. Bring to a boil, cover with a lid, reduce the heat and simmer for 50 minutes.

Add the daikon and onion, cover with the lid, and simmer for another 50 minutes, by which time the meat will be meltingly tender and the gravy dark and glossy. Serve with boiled rice.

# MANCHURIAN-STYLE STEAK
# 滿洲牛扒

🌾 *Gluten free*

❤ *Dairy free*

◐ *Egg free*

*Serves 2*

*Preparation time 15 minutes*

*Cooking time 15 minutes*

**12oz beef tenderloin, cut into 1-inch**
   **thick pieces**

**2 tablespoons vegetable oil**

*For the marinade*

**1 teaspoon salt**

**1 teaspoon sugar**

**2 tablespoons potato starch**

**2 tablespoons water**

*For the black pepper sauce*

**1 tablespoon vegetable oil**

**1 medium onion, finely sliced**

**1 garlic clove, minced**

**1 tablespoon black peppercorns**

**¼ cup beef or chicken stock**
   *(see page 12)*

**1 teaspoon Shaoxing rice wine**

**1 medium green pepper, finely sliced**

**1 teaspoon salt**

**1 teaspoon sugar**

**\*Lisa's tips**

*Make sure the sauce is ready before cooking
the steak.*

Our family's history has had its ups and downs, and I am not proud to say that my grandfather had associations with the Triads. The term "Triad" was given by the Hong Kong government to Chinese secret societies and it is based on the triangular symbol that once represented such societies—the Chinese character "hung," encased in a triangle, symbolizing the union of heaven, earth, and man.

The commonly accepted myth about Triads is that their members were a resistance movement set up by five monks who went on to establish five monasteries and five secret societies. Known as the Shaolin Monks, their mission was to overthrow the Manchu emperors—who had taken China's northern capital (Peking) by force in around 1674 to establish the Qing Dynasty—and to restore the Ming Dynasty, which was seen as the golden age of China. Although they were Buddhist monks, these rebels ate this beef dish to give them strength and counter the harsh weather.

METHOD

First marinate the steak. Put it in a shallow bowl, add the salt, sugar, potato starch, and water, and combine well. Set aside to marinate for 10 minutes; this will help to soften the steak and retain its juiciness.

Meanwhile, make the sauce. Heat a saucepan on high heat and add 1 tablespoon of oil. Drop in the onion and cook for about 3 minutes until browned. Add the garlic, peppercorns, and stock, and bring to a boil. Boil rapidly until the liquid has reduced by one-third. Pour in the Shaoxing wine, add the peppers, and bring to a boil. Season with salt and sugar and remove from the heat; set aside.

Add 2 tablespoons of oil to a hot wok and pan-fry the steak for 3–4 minutes on each side, or until cooked to your liking. Add the black pepper sauce and heat through until bubbling.

# YEEP'S STEAMED BEEF MEATBALLS ON WILTED NAPA CABBAGE
時菜牛肉球

*Gluten free*

*Dairy free*

*Egg free*

*Serves 2 (Makes approx. 10–15 meatballs)*

*Preparation time 25 minutes*

*Cooking time 15 minutes*

¾ cup water chestnuts, finely diced

2 tablespoons orange zest

1 teaspoon grated fresh ginger

8oz ground beef

1 teaspoon salt

1 teaspoon sugar

½ teaspoon sesame oil

½ teaspoon white pepper

2 tablespoons water

2 tablespoons potato starch

½ cup fresh cilantro leaves, finely
    chopped

2 Napa cabbage leaves

barbecue sauce, to serve *(see page 15)*

*Lisa's tips

*This is THE Chinese meatball recipe—the water chestnuts give this dish a lightness that other meatballs can only dream of!*

Our grandmother is one of six girls and the third oldest. The eldest sister, Yeep (short for Yee Pore), was a formidable woman who, like our grandmother, came to the UK and cooked. Yeep spent the last years of her life in a nursing home and often called on me to cook for her because she was frustrated by the lack of Chinese food on offer. Yeep surprised me one day by telephoning. When I picked up the phone and heard her calling to me in a raspy voice, my heart sank. "I'm dying," she said. But then Yeep continued, "Before I do… bring me some meatballs… and some of your barbecue sauce." She cracked me up. Right away I cooked some steaming meatballs and took them over for her to enjoy, and as she ate them she gained strength and smiled at me fondly. There is nothing more satisfying in the world than to eat your favorite food, and I am honored to include this dish that Yeep loved so much.

The meatballs are steamed over Napa cabbage, rather than fried, to keep them moist and succulent.

METHOD

First make the meatballs. Tip the water chestnuts into a bowl and stir in the orange zest and grated ginger. Add the ground beef and mix together until well blended. Season with salt, sugar, sesame oil, and white pepper. Add the water and mix to a paste, and then add the potato starch and chopped cilantro. Cover the bowl with plastic wrap and transfer the mixture to the fridge to firm up for 10 minutes.

Separate the Napa cabbage leaves and place them side by side on a heatproof plate. Using an ice-cream scoop or spoon, scoop the meatball mixture into 10–15 balls and arrange them on the Chinese leaves.

To cook the meatballs, transfer the plate to a preheated steamer and steam the meatballs for 15 minutes until they become firm to the touch. If you don't have a steamer, use your wok (see page 127).

Remove the meatballs from the steamer and serve them with some barbecue sauce on the side.

# ASIAN-STYLE BURGER (Iron Chef contender)
# 亞洲漢堡包

*Use gluten-free flour and Worcestershire sauce. Replace the oyster sauce with tamari.*

*Dairy free*

*Egg free*

Serves 2 (Makes 8)
Preparation time 45 minutes
Cooking time 30 minutes

**For the mantou buns**

**2 cups all-purpose flour**

**½ cup water**

**1 teaspoon baking powder**

**½ tablespoon yeast**

**⅓ cup sugar**

*For the burger*

**10oz good-quality lean ground beef**

**pinch of salt**

**pinch of sugar**

**pinch of white pepper**

**dash of oyster sauce**

**dried zest of 1 orange**

**dash of Worcestershire sauce**

**2 teaspoons Shaoxing rice wine**

**1 tablespoon potato starch**

**¾ cup water chestnuts, finely chopped**

**a handful of cilantro, chopped**

**1 teaspoon sesame oil**

**1 tablespoon vegetable oil**

*For the beet relish*

**2 cooked beets, finely chopped**

**½ white onion, finely chopped**

**pinch of salt**

**2 teaspoons sugar**

**1 tablespoon white vinegar**

**a handful of flatleaf parsley, chopped**

**½ tablespoon olive oil**

I cooked this dish on TV for the prestigious program *Iron Chef*, which originated in Japan. Its American version has gained cult status as well as the blessing of Michelle Obama, who invited *Iron Chef* to the White House. The theme of the show is to cook a dish in one hour using a secret ingredient that is only revealed to the contender at the start of the show. The Japanese phrase for this is *omakase*; I call it "omigod!"

When I appeared on the show, the secret ingredient was beets. This isn't an ingredient that often appears in Chinese cuisine, but beets go perfectly with beef. So, thinking on my feet, I came up with this recipe. Thankfully, the *Iron Chef* judges loved it and, given the crazy, zany mood on the show, I loved cooking it, too.

METHOD

To make the mantou buns, combine all the ingredients in a bowl and knead together to form a soft dough. Cover the bowl with plastic wrap and set aside at room temperature for approx. 15 minutes or until doubled in size. Divide the dough into 8 equal pieces and shape into round balls, approx. 1-inch in diameter. Arrange the buns on an oiled baking sheet, cover with a towel, and set aside to rise in a warm place for about 15 minutes.

To cook the buns, put them in a preheated steamer and steam for 10 minutes. (For instructions on how to steam in a wok, see page 127.) Transfer them to a wire rack to cool.

To make the burgers, put all the ingredients except the vegetable oil in a large bowl and mix well with your hands to combine. Shape into 8 neat patties, 1 inch in diameter, and arrange on a plate. Cover with plastic wrap and transfer to the fridge to firm up for 20 minutes.

To make the relish, combine the beets and onion in a bowl with the salt, sugar, vinegar, parsley, and olive oil. Check the seasoning, adding more salt or sugar if needed.

To cook the burgers, heat the oil over high heat in a frying pan. Cook the burgers for 4–5 minutes on each side or until cooked to your liking.
To serve, halve the mantou buns, add the burgers, and accompany with lettuce, tomato, and beet relish.

# ERIC'S LOVE OFFERING OF STEAK AND LEEK STIR FRY
## 韭菜炒牛柳

*Use tamari rather than soy sauce.*
*Omit the oyster sauce.*

*Dairy free*

*Egg free*

*Serves 2*

*Preparation time 15 minutes*

*Cooking time 15 minutes*

5 tablespoons vegetable oil

10oz sirloin steak, thinly sliced

1 garlic clove, minced

1 leek, washed thoroughly and
    cut into thin strips approx.
    2-inches in length

1 medium onion, finely sliced

½ cup beef stock

1 teaspoon oyster sauce

1 drop of dark soy sauce

pinch of salt

pinch of sugar

2 tablespoons potato starch mixture
    *(see page 8)*

1 teaspoon sesame oil

*Lisa's tips
Make sure that you open up the leeks and
wash them thoroughly since sometimes
there can be dirt hidden within.*

Our mother met Eric, our dad, back in the 1970s. When she saw him at the airport for the first time with his shaggy hair and thick black glasses, it was love at first sight. However, Eric had to go on proposing for weeks afterward before she could take him seriously. It was only when Eric made this dish for our mother, using the choicest steak he could afford, that she said yes. So perhaps the old adage is true, the way to the heart is through the stomach.

This recipe is a great way to liven up sirloin steak. It is very easy to make, but delicious—with varying layers of sweetness from the leeks, onions, and steak.

METHOD

Add the oil to a hot wok, put in the raw steak slices, and stir-fry over high heat for about 5 minutes until cooked to your liking. Remove the steak from the wok and set aside on a plate to rest. Pour off the excess oil from the wok.

Return the wok to high heat—it should still be lightly coated in oil—and stir-fry the garlic, leek, and onion for 1 minute. Return the cooked steak to the pan, pour in the stock, and add the oyster sauce and dark soy sauce. Season with salt and sugar. Bring the sauce to a boil, add the potato starch mixture, and stir vigorously to thicken the dish. Finish with a splash of sesame oil. Serve with rice or noodles.

# HONG KONG BEEF SKEWERS WITH SATAY DIP

## 串燒牛肉沙嗲

*Serves 2*
*Preparation time 30 minutes*
*Cooking time 15 minutes*

**7oz beef tenderloin, cut into thin strips**

**12 x 7-inch bamboo skewers, soaked in warm water for 30 minutes**

*For the marinade*

**1 tablespoon sesame oil**

**1 tablespoon Shaoxing rice wine or sherry**

**1 tablespoon light soy sauce**

**½ teaspoon salt**

**½ teaspoon sugar**

**½ teaspoon minced garlic**

*For the satay dip*

**1 cup raw, unsalted peanuts**

**½ teaspoon salt**

**½ teaspoon ground turmeric**

**½ teaspoon chile paste**

**1 tablespoon brown sugar**

**2 tablespoons water**

**1 tablespoon vegetable oil**

**\*Lisa's tips**

*Soak the skewers in warm water for 30 minutes to stop them from burning. This dish can be cooked in the oven, on a grill pan, or over a barbecue.*

A family reunion in Hong Kong in 2002 exposed a huge divide between our two cultures and countries—and yet it was this visit that inspired my sister and me to return to our roots and open our Sweet Mandarin restaurant. From the outset, the differences were apparent for all to see. Our family stood in a line on the sidewalk, open-mouthed and out of place. Our aunt took us to Ladies' Market, where they sold ladies' clothes, but I felt enormous next to the people around me—like Gulliver, surrounded by the tiny inhabitants of a Far Eastern Lilliput. It was clear that while we were ethnically Chinese, we dressed and looked totally different from the native Hong Kong people.

In my dismay at not being able to shop for clothes, my attention turned to food, and I soon discovered rows of hawker stalls selling skewered meats. I made a beeline for the beef skewers and, as I raised the meat to my lips, all the anxiety I initially felt about our cultural differences disappeared. My raison d'être was the food; here I had found a little piece of the jigsaw. My goal in Hong Kong became clear—I was here to rediscover my roots, learn the culinary delights of the locals, and bring them home to share with my customers. These beef skewers are a perfect starter; the satay dip makes them extra special.

METHOD

Mix together the ingredients for the marinade in a bowl, add the steak, and combine. Set aside to marinate in the fridge for at least 20 minutes.

Meanwhile, prepare the satay dip. Crush the peanuts using a mortar and pestle (or put them in a plastic bag and crush with a rolling pin). You want to retain some texture in the sauce so do not blend the peanuts in a food processor, which will crush them to a pulp. Pour the peanuts into a dry frying pan and toast over low heat for 2 minutes or until they turn golden brown. Add the salt, turmeric, chile paste, and sugar, and cook for another 2 minutes. Add the water and oil and cook for 5 minutes.

Preheat a grill pan. Thread the marinated beef onto the wooden skewers and grill for 3 minutes on each side or until cooked to your liking. Serve with the satay sauce.

I remember watching our parents and grandmother pick their fish and how they would comment if one was not fresh. Their ability to know instinctively which was the freshest fish always amazed me. Here are some tips for sourcing the freshest fish and seafood:

Look at the fish's eyes—they should be clear and bulge slightly. If the eyes are indented or cloudy then don't buy.

Fish filets and steaks should be moist and without any yellow or brown discoloration.

Whole fish or filleted fish should have firm and shiny flesh. Avoid if the flesh appears dull.

Check the gills—they should be a nice bright red and free from slime.

The fish should smell mild—more like the sea than fishy. If it smells fishy, the fish has probably been there a while and is not very fresh.

The versatility of fish is highlighted in this chapter as dishes vary from steamed sea bass to a hearty fish casserole. The recipes use all types of fish and the majority of dishes are made using fish filets, which saves time cleaning and filleting. Try the Steamed Soy Sauce Scallops (page 124), which are like morsels of heaven, or the Celebration Lobster Noodles (see page 129) for special occasions. Seafood dishes are great for stir-frying, but it is important not to overcook them, especially shrimp or squid, which become rubbery if cooked for too long.

魚和海鮮

# FISH & SEAFOOD

# CANTONESE STEAMED FISH WITH GINGER AND SCALLION
## 清蒸海上鮮

*Use tamari rather than soy sauce.*

*Dairy free*

*Egg free*

*Serves 2*

*Preparation time 10 minutes*

*Cooking time 20 minutes*

**1 whole white fish (such as sea bass), weighing approx. 1 lb, scaled and gutted**

**1 onion, finely sliced**

**1 teaspoon salt**

**1-inch piece of fresh ginger, peeled and finely sliced**

**3 scallions, finely sliced**

**2 tablespoons vegetable oil**

**2 tablespoons light soy sauce**

\*Lisa's tips

*Lemon sole is a great alternative to sea bass for this dish.*

Our grandmother used to go fishing with her father when she was a child and fondly remembers how she used to ride to the lake on the back of his bicycle—no one had cars in those days. When they arrived back home, the fish would still be jumping and gasping for air; they were that fresh. In China it is traditional to serve fish with the head and tail on, as a symbol of abundance—however, you could always use filets of fish for this instead.

METHOD

Score the fish on an angle from head to tail, approx. 1 inch apart, making sure that the cuts are not too deep. Scatter the onion over a heatproof plate, lay the whole fish on top, and season with salt.

Put the fish, on its plate, inside a preheated steamer and steam for 15 minutes (if you don't have a steamer, see page 127 for how to convert your wok into a steamer). Remove the fish from the steamer and transfer it to a serving plate, discarding the sliced onions.

Add the oil to a hot wok and set over high heat. Throw in the ginger and scallions and give them a quick stir. Pour this oil over the fish. Splash the soy sauce over the fish and serve.

# SALMON WITH SWEET SOY
# 醬汁三文魚

*Use tamari rather than soy sauce. Check the mirin does not contain hydrolysed vegetable protein (HVP), which may be made from wheat. If it does, replace with sake or dry sherry with some sugar.*

*Dairy free*

*Egg free*

*Serves 2*

*Preparation time 20 minutes*

*Cooking time 15 minutes*

**½ cup sake**

**1 cup mirin**

**½ cup Japanese soy sauce (*shoyu*)**

**2 tablespoons brown sugar**

**2 tablespoons vegetable oil**

**2 x 4oz salmon filets**

**2 scallions, finely sliced**

**½-inch piece of fresh ginger, peeled and sliced**

**\*Lisa's tips**

*You can substitute tuna for salmon if you wish. Both salmon and tuna are a good source of omega 3 (something the body cannot naturally produce), which is needed for maintaining the cells that regulate blood clotting, body temperature, blood pressure, and immune function.*

This dish is dedicated to my great-grandfather, Leung, who manufactured soy sauce and whose favorite fish was salmon. Although I never met this formidable man, it was his endeavors that inspired me to launch our sauce business and keep the family dream alive. We make this dish every year in memory of my great-grandfather during the spring Qingming festival, when we head to the burial ground with incense, paper money, and food offerings to appease our hungry ancestors and give them currency in the afterlife.

METHOD

Combine the sake, mirin, soy sauce, and sugar in a small saucepan and heat over high heat, stirring. Bring to a boil, reduce the heat, and simmer for approx. 15 minutes until the sauce thickens. Remove from the heat and set aside.

Heat the oil in a wok over high heat. Add the salmon filets and cook for 5 minutes on each side. Pour the sauce into the wok and cook for another 5 minutes.

To serve, sprinkle the scallions and ginger over the salmon and accompany with a large helping of boiled rice.

# SWEET CHILE COD ON A BED OF NOODLES
## 甜辣椒鱈魚麵

Use gluten-free noodles (see page 156).

Dairy free

Serves 2

Preparation time 10 minutes

Cooking time 20 minutes

**2 x 6oz cod filets**

**a few pinches of salt**

**1¼ cups sweet chile sauce**

(see page 14)

**5oz dried fine egg noodles**

**1 tablespoon vegetable oil**

**1 medium onion, finely sliced**

**1½ cups finely shredded cabbage**

**1 teaspoon sugar**

**½ teaspoon sesame oil**

*****Lisa's tips**

*Do your bit for the world and use sustainably caught cod—look out for the blue Marine Stewardship Council (MSC) logo when you are buying it.*

I am passionate about passing on my cooking skills and food knowledge to the next generation. I love seeing students master new culinary skills—it's cathartic—and I am delighted that Manchester City Council has endorsed my work, making Sweet Mandarin the specialist food education provider to 174 local schools. Currently I teach at about two schools a day during the school year. The program varies, depending on the age of the children, but the message stays the same—to educate students about real food, not processed stuff, and demonstrate how delicious it is.

During a cooking lesson with a local school, I was shocked to discover that 18 out of the 20 students had never tasted fish before. Noodles were popular, sweet chile was super-popular, but fish… urgh! Armed with this information, I set out to change this depressing fact and came up with this recipe for Sweet Chile Cod on a Bed of Noodles. The result? They all tried my dish and loved it! So this recipe had to be included—for future generations of students and to show the power of food.

METHOD

Preheat the oven to 350°F.

Season the cod filets with a pinch of salt on both sides. Arrange them on a foil-lined baking sheet and pour on the Sweet Chile Sauce. Bake in the oven for 10 minutes. Switch off the heat and leave the cod to rest in the oven until you are ready to serve.

Meanwhile, bring a pan of water to a boil, add the noodles, and set aside to soak, off the heat, for 5 minutes. Drain, refresh under cold running water, and set aside.

Heat a wok over high heat and add the oil. Put in the onion and cabbage and stir-fry until soft, approx. 5 minutes. Add the cooked noodles to the pan and toss well for about a minute until heated through. Season with a pinch of salt, the sugar, and the sesame oil.

To serve, portion out the noodles onto two plates. Remove the fish from the pan, arrange one fillet on top of each pile of noodles, and spoon on the warm sauce.

# SALT AND CHILE FISH
# 椒鹽魚塊

● *Gluten free*

♥ *Dairy free*

*Serves 2*

*Preparation time 15 minutes*

*Cooking time 15 minutes*

**2 x 4oz filets of cod or grouper,**
   **cut into 1-inch chunks**

**1 teaspoon salt**

**1 egg, beaten**

**¾ cup potato starch**

**3 tablespoons vegetable oil**

**2 garlic cloves, finely chopped**

**1 long fresh red chile, finely chopped**

**½ green pepper, finely diced**

**½ onion, finely chopped**

**½ teaspoon sugar**

**½ teaspoon five spice powder**

**2 tablespoons Shaoxing rice wine**

**\*Lisa's tips**

*For an extra special version of this dish
try monkfish, which has the same texture
as lobster. If you want some heat, add
½ teaspoon of chile flakes or half a fresh
red chile.*

I grew up in a take-out restaurant and every Friday night we would have a line of people ordering fish and chips. It's a pressure-cooker environment; you're inches away from the customers who are watching your every move in the open plan kitchen/serving area. Our parents don't work well together and have clear boundaries: Dad looked after the kitchen and Chinese dishes; Mom looked after the fryers at the front and served the customers fish and chips. Unfortunately, they argue like cat and dog. Even though their arguments were always about little things, when I was growing up it felt like the whole town knew about the "Punch and Judy Show" being played out inside our restaurant. Men usually sided with Dad ("Poor Eric!") while women would side with Mom ("Is Eric at it again, Mabel? If so, fire him!"). Typical disagreements were over the lengthy time Dad took to cook a dish or if Mom gave a customer too many french fries. One day, the bickering was going at full force just as Mom was lifting a piece of fish out of the fryer. Mom was angry at Dad because he had forgotten her portion of onions, so she started wagging the fish at him… it fell out of her hands and broke into pieces on the counter. Another argument ensued about the fact the fish had broken, whose fault it was, and how the customer would now have to wait for another fish. When service was over, not wanting to waste the broken fish, I remember how Dad cleverly turned it into salt and chile fish pieces, which tasted even more delicious than the initial dish—giving me comfort that even when things are broken, they can still be put together again.

METHOD

Season the fish pieces with ½ teaspoon of salt. Drop the fish first into the beaten egg and then into the potato starch to coat it.

Heat a wok with 2 tablespoons of oil over medium heat. Add the fish and cook for 5 minutes on each side until golden brown. Remove from the wok and set aside to drain on paper towels.

Clean the wok and return it to high heat with 1 tablespoon of oil. Add the garlic, chile, pepper, and onion, and stir-fry for 2 minutes. Return the crispy fish to the pan and season with ½ teaspoon of salt, the sugar, and the five spice powder. Add the Shaoxing wine and toss well.

# HEARTY FISH CASSEROLE
# 魚肉煲

- Use tamari rather than oyster sauce.
- Dairy free
- Egg free

Serves 2
Preparation time 15 minutes
Cooking time 15 minutes

**14oz grouper, cut into chunky pieces**

**2 tablespoons vegetable oil**

**4oz tofu, cut into 1-inch squares**

**2 garlic cloves, finely sliced**

**1-inch piece of fresh ginger,**
**peeled and finely sliced**

**5 Chinese mushrooms, soaked in**
**boiling water for 15 minutes**
**then halved**

**4 baby corns, sliced lengthwise**

**1 Napa cabbage, cut into**
**bite-sized pieces**

**1 carrot, peeled and sliced into**
**rounds**

**¾ cup chicken stock** *(see page 12)*

**1 teaspoon salt, plus extra for**
**seasoning the fish**

**1 teaspoon sugar**

**1 teaspoon oyster sauce**

**1 teaspoon sesame oil**

**1 teaspoon Shaoxing rice wine**

**2 teaspoons potato starch mixture**
*(see page 8)*

**\*Lisa's tips**

*This is delicious reheated the next day, by which time the flavorsome sauce will have soaked into the fish and vegetables, making them even tastier.*

This is a family recipe that my great-grandmother, Tai Po, used to make for my mother and uncle when they were in her care while their mother, our grandmother, came to England to work. My mother remembers how this dish was a firm favorite with Tai Po because it was quick and easy to make and could be reheated again for dinner. Tai Po was a no-nonsense woman who measured every ingredient down to the last yen to make ends meet. This dish was filled to the brim with odds and ends of fish and bulked up with Chinese vegetables.

METHOD

Season the fish with salt and set aside.

Heat a wok over high heat and add the oil. Pan-fry the tofu for 3 minutes until firm and crispy. Add the garlic, ginger, and vegetables, and cook for 3 minutes, stirring carefully so the tofu doesn't break up.

Pour in the chicken stock, nestle the pieces of fish in the pan, and season with salt, sugar, oyster sauce, sesame oil, and Shaoxing wine. Bring to a boil and simmer gently for 15 minutes until the fish is cooked through. Bring the sauce back to a boil and add the potato starch mixture, stirring vigorously to thicken the sauce.

# SESAME TUNA SKEWERS
# 芝麻串燒吞拿魚

 Use tamari rather than hoisin sauce.

 Dairy free

 Egg free

*Serves 2*

*Preparation time 40 minutes*

*Cooking time 10 minutes*

**8oz tuna steak, cut into 2-inch cubes**

**1 large onion, cut into wedges**

**2 small red peppers, cut into ½-inch dice**

**2 tablespoons hoisin sauce**

**1 teaspoon sesame oil**

**1 tablespoon Shaoxing rice wine**

**1 tablespoon toasted sesame seeds**

**\*Lisa's tips**

*Don't marinate the tuna for longer than 30 minutes, or the acid in the vinegar will break down the protein in the fish and it will come apart more easily when cooked.*

"You've just spent what on a fish?," I asked Kiyoshi Kimura, the owner of Sushi Zanmai.

"155 million yen… on a tuna," he replied laughing.

"You're joking," I said shocked.

"No. I bought a tuna for $1.5 million at the auction. I won the bid! I don't joke around when it comes to fish."

Silence from my end. Could it be true? A single bluefin tuna bought for $1.5 million?

"Wow, congratulations Kiyoshi," I said and hung up the phone—stunned.

You might have read about this incredible yet true story in the papers in 2013 when Sushi Zanmai, the Japanese restaurant chain, paid $1.5 million for Daisuke Takeuchi's 490 lb tuna, which he caught in the odd-sounding coastal town of Ooma-cho. Although the restaurant lost more than 100 million yen dividing the fish up into 10,000 pieces of tuna sashimi, I was told they bought the tuna first because it was top quality and second to demonstrate to the world how much they value tuna. In his defense, Kimura-san said it was worth it for the free press coverage he received.

Thankfully, tuna isn't that expensive at the supermarket, and the good news is that it's a rich source of omega-3 fatty acids. It's a great fish to use for sushi, but it is also delicious cooked. In this recipe, the meaty flavor works beautifully with the sesame seeds.

METHOD

Soak 6 wooden skewers, 2 inches in length, in warm water for 30 minutes. Thread the tuna, onion, and pepper onto the skewers, allowing two pieces of tuna per skewer. Arrange on a plate and set aside.

Mix together the hoisin sauce, sesame oil, and Shaoxing wine in a bowl. Brush the mixture over the skewers, cover with plastic wrap, and transfer to the fridge to marinate for 30 minutes.

Preheat the broiler to medium-high, arrange the skewers on a broiler pan, and cook under the hot broiler for 3–4 minutes on each side. Sprinkle with toasted sesame seeds.

# PAN-FRIED SHRIMP AND TOMATO SAUCE
## 番茄大蝦

*Replace the soy sauce with tamari.*

*Dairy free*

*Egg free*

*Serves 2*

*Preparation time 10 minutes*

*Cooking time 15 minutes*

**8oz raw shrimp, shell on**

**1 tablespoon vegetable oil**

**2 garlic cloves, finely chopped**

**1 teaspoon salt**

**1 teaspoon sugar**

**1 teaspoon light soy sauce**

**1 teaspoon Shaoxing rice wine**

**1 tablespoon tomato paste**

**½ cup chicken stock** *(see page 12)*

**2 scallions, finely sliced**

**3 teaspoons potato starch mixture**
  *(see page 8)*

**\*Lisa's tips**

*Tomatoes and shrimp are a match made in heaven. If you don't feel like peeling the shells, then you can use raw shrimp that have already been peeled.*

This is a dish that oozes love. I came up with the recipe especially for our Valentine's Day menu as a dish that lovers could share—lightly battered shrimp, resembling hearts, dipped in a sweet, naughty Peking-style sauce. I remember watching as couples bit into the shrimp, which oozed flavor, and how excitement levels became instantly electric—in fact, the dish created such an amazing energy at Sweet Mandarin that night we had to tell some diners to cool it down! Go on, dim the lights and watch this dish make your partner blush!

METHOD

Remove the legs from the shrimp with scissors. Make an opening in the back of each shrimp and devein, leaving the shell and tail on for added flavor.

Heat a wok over high heat and add the oil. Stir-fry the garlic for 1 minute to flavor the oil. Add the shrimp and stir-fry for 5 minutes or until they change color from translucent white to deep pinky-red. Season with salt, sugar, soy sauce, and Shaoxing wine. Add the tomato paste and mix. Pour in the chicken stock and stir well to create a tomato sauce.

Add the scallions, bring the sauce to a boil, and stir in the potato starch mixture to thicken.

# SWEET CHILE SHRIMP
# 甜辣大蝦

*Gluten free*

*Dairy free*

*Egg free*

*Serves 2*

*Preparation time 10 minutes*

*Cooking time 15 minutes*

**4 asparagus spears, chopped into
1-inch lengths**

**8oz raw, peeled shrimp,
deveined, tail on**

**salt**

**1 tablespoon vegetable oil**

**½-inch piece of fresh ginger,
peeled and sliced**

**1 onion, finely sliced**

**2 scallions, cut into 1-inch lengths**

**1¼ cups sweet chile sauce**

*(see page 14)*

*Lisa's tips

*This is a really easy dish to make for a
quick supper. Running the asparagus
under cold water keeps it bright green
and crunchy.*

My mother told me this dish would be our inheritance, the living part of our family tree, and she taught me how to make it as part of my birthright. It seemed as if schoolwork and life's other little frustrations all seemed to evaporate as we sat down to enjoy it. My mother always used to say, "this dish tantalizes the tastebuds and the eyes"—and she was absolutely right.

METHOD

Blanch the asparagus in boiling water for 3 minutes; drain, refresh under cold running water, and set aside.

Season the shrimp all over with a light sprinkling of salt. Heat a wok over high heat and add the oil. Put in the ginger, sliced onion, scallions, and cooked asparagus and stir-fry for 2 minutes.

Add the shrimp and continue to stir-fry for another 5–7 minutes or until the shrimp turn a vibrant pink color. Pour in the sweet chile sauce, toss well to combine, and bring briefly to a boil. Serve with steamed rice.

# POACHED CRAYFISH WITH A SWEET AND SPICY DIP

## 水煮小龍蝦

*Gluten free*

*Dairy free*

*Egg free*

*Serves 2*

*Preparation time 5 minutes*

*Cooking time 10 minutes*

**1-inch piece of fresh ginger,
peeled and roughly chopped**

**2 garlic cloves, peeled but kept whole**

**1 red chile, roughly chopped**

**1 teaspoon sugar**

**1 teaspoon salt**

**1 tablespoon Shaoxing rice wine**

**juice of ½ lime**

**20 large live crayfish**

\*Lisa's tips

*Fresh crayfish should have their legs and antennae intact and their eyes should be black.*

I first came across crayfish when Dad brought a bucket load of them home from the fish market. As children we used to call them "baby lobsters" and thought they were a great novelty with their individual antennae, little claws, and pincers. I remember how we used to charge around the kitchen play-fighting with them—that is, until Dad told us off for messing around and confiscated our live weapons.

Crayfish are sometimes seen as a poor relation to lobster and their tails are often breaded and sold as scampi. However, I think that their distinctive, sweet flavor should really be appreciated in its own right and, for me, this dish showcases that delicate flavor beautifully.

METHOD

For the sweet and spicy dip, add the ginger, garlic, chile, sugar, salt, Shaoxing wine, and lime juice to a mortar and crush with a pestle until combined.

For the crayfish, fill a large saucepan with water and bring to a boil. Add the live crayfish and cook for 3–4 minutes until the seafood turns bright pinky red and the tails start to curve around. Drain through a colander, discarding the stock, and transfer the crayfish to a serving dish.

Serve the crayfish while they are still hot with the sweet and spicy dip on the side. First suck out all the juices from the shells, then peel off the shells with your fingers (the shells are easy to break), dunk in the dip, and enjoy the sweet chile flesh.

# SHANGHAI SHRIMP
# 上海大蝦

- ❶ *Use tamari rather than soy sauce.*
- ♥ *Dairy free*
- ◐ *Egg free*

*Serves 2*
*Preparation time 10 minutes*
*Cooking time 15 minutes*

**4oz medium, raw large shrimp,
shell on**
**4 tablespoons vegetable oil**
**½-inch piece of fresh ginger,
peeled and finely chopped**
**3 scallions, cut into 1-inch lengths**
**2 tablespoons dry sherry**
**4 tablespoons dark soy sauce**
**3 tablespoons sugar**
**2 teaspoons red wine vinegar**

**\*Lisa's tips**
*The sherry gives a freshness to the shrimp,
while the ginger provides some heat to
liven them up.*

This dish is finger-licking good—a delicious blend of meaty shrimp, fresh ginger, and sweet, syrupy sauce. I first tasted it during a trip to Shanghai. I was suffering from jetlag at the time and I remember how the flavors revived me instantly—in fact, I was so taken with the dish I failed to notice that a fight had broken out only a few tables away, which quickly emptied the restaurant. Luckily the police arrived and, as they blew on their whistles, the men fled—some scrambling up a nearby ladder, the rest darting into the warren of alleys. Meanwhile, I sat transfixed, savoring every drop of the sweet, glossy sauce. I was numb with tiredness from my long plane journey, but my adrenalin was pumping—not because of the fight, but because the dish was so absolutely delicious. I finished it all, licking my fingers afterward.

METHOD
Remove the legs from the shrimp with scissors. Make an opening in the back of each shrimp and devein, leaving the shell and tail on.

Heat the oil in a saucepan or wok over high heat. Reduce the heat to low and stir-fry the ginger and scallions for 30 seconds to release their flavor into the oil. Increase the heat to high, add the shrimp, and stir-fry for 1 minute until they change from translucent white to bright pinky-red. Add the remaining ingredients and stir-fry for about 2 minutes until the sauce is glazed.

Serve hot or at room temperature.

# SCALLOPS WITH GINGER AND SCALLIONS
## 姜葱大蝦

 Use tamari rather than soy sauce.

♥ Dairy free

○ Egg free

Serves 2

Preparation time 10 minutes

Cooking time 10 minutes

**2 tablespoons vegetable oil**

**1-inch piece of fresh ginger,**
**peeled and finely sliced**

**7oz large sea scallops**
**(approx. 10), roes on if available,**
**but without the shells**

**2 scallions, finely sliced**

**1 teaspoon minced garlic**

**⅔ cup chicken stock** *(see page 12)*

**1 teaspoon salt**

**1 teaspoon sugar**

**1 teaspoon sesame oil**

**2 teaspoons Shaoxing rice wine**

**½ teaspoon light soy sauce**

**2 tablespoons potato starch mixture**
*(see page 8)*

**\*Lisa's tips**

*The holy trinity of Chinese cooking is ginger,*
*garlic, and scallions. This dish is a little bit of*
*heaven on a scallop!*

I love eating scallops as an appetizer and often serve them as a treat. I find their delicate flavor and firm but springy texture goes perfectly with ginger and scallion, which aren't too strong in flavor and don't overwhelm their subtle sweetness.

To do your bit for Mother Nature, buy from producers who don't use the destructive dredging method.

METHOD

Heat a wok over high heat and add the oil. Sauté the ginger for 2 minutes to infuse into the oil. Add the scallops and cook for 2–3 minutes on each side or until the flesh becomes firm.

Add the scallions and garlic and stir-fry for 1 minute. Pour in the stock and season with salt, sugar, sesame oil, Shaoxing wine, and soy sauce. Once the sauce is bubbling, add the potato starch mixture, stirring vigorously to thicken the sauce.

# STEAMED SOY SAUCE SCALLOPS
## 醬汁蒸帶子

*Use tamari rather than soy sauce.*

*Dairy free*

*Egg free*

*Serves 2*

*Preparation time 18 minutes*

*Cooking time 18 minutes*

**10 large scallops in their shells**

**1 teaspoon salt**

**1 teaspoon sugar**

**2oz rice vermicelli noodles**

**10 teaspoons dried minced garlic or garlic granules**

**2 scallions, finely sliced**

**2 tablespoons vegetable oil**

**splash of light soy sauce**

### *Lisa's tips

*The rice vermicelli absorbs all the juices from the scallops—delicious! If you don't have any scallop shells, you can always put the scallops on individual saucers instead.*

On Sundays our father, Eric, likes to sit quietly reading the papers and pretends not to pay much attention to our mother, Mabel. But in his heyday, he was quite a Romeo and drove Mabel to different parts of the UK to "see the world." One year he decided to take her to Scotland since she had never tried scallops before. He was keen to dive for the scallops himself, so he convinced an old fisherman to take them out into the North Sea. The only problem was that Eric couldn't actually swim (although he didn't want Mabel to know that). When the fisherman shouted jump, Eric hefted himself up on trembling arms. Whispering a silent prayer to his ancestors, he levered himself over the rail and out into the cold, icy air. As he plunged into the water, the saltiness stung his eyes and Eric started to flap in shock. The old fisherman grinned and, hauling him out of the water, congratulated himself on "the big catch" he'd just made. Although Eric's efforts were in vain, the fisherman took pity on him and gave him a bagful of scallops, thanking him for the amusing experience. Today, whenever we make this dish at home, my mother laughs and laughs—meanwhile, my father rolls his eyes and returns to his newspaper.

METHOD

Remove the scallops and the roes from the shells, discarding the membrane that surrounds them. Rinse under cold running water and pat dry on paper towels. Put the scallops back in their shells and season with salt and sugar.

Soak the noodles in cold water for 3 minutes; drain thoroughly. Using a fork, twist the noodles into 10 little nests and put one nest on top of each scallop. Sprinkle a teaspoon of dried minced garlic over the top of each nest.

Put the assembled scallop shells inside a preheated steamer and steam for 10 minutes; you might have to cook them in batches depending on the size of your pan. The scallops are cooked when they change color from translucent pale pink to opaque white and are firm to the touch.

Remove the scallops from the steamer and sprinkle on the scallions.

To serve, heat the oil in a wok over high heat and drizzle it over the scallops—the hot oil will cook the scallions and seal the scallop edges. Drizzle with soy sauce to serve.

# HOW TO CONVERT YOUR WOK INTO A STEAMER

To turn your wok into a steamer, put a wire cake rack inside the wok and pour in boiling water so it is just under the level of the rack. Set the wok over high heat until the water comes to a boil. Meanwhile, place your food on a heatproof plate. Carefully lower the plate onto the rack inside the wok, cover with a lid and steam as required.

The image on the left shows a conventional bamboo steamer with two layers and a lid, which allows you to steam two different dishes at the same time. Fill the steamer with the dishes and put it into a wok filled with sufficient water to come approx. one-third of the way up the sides of the steamer.

# FRIED SCALLOPS WITH CHINESE SAUSAGE
## 臘腸炒帶子

*Gluten free*

*Dairy free*

*Egg free*

Serves 2

*Preparation time 10 minutes*

*Cooking time 10 minutes*

**1 tablespoon vegetable oil**

**1 Chinese sausage (*lap cheong*),**
  **thinly sliced**

**12 large scallops, roes on if available**
  **but without the shells**

**pinch of salt**

**2 scallions, finely sliced**

### *Lisa's tips

*Scallops and Chinese sausage go extremely well together. If you haven't got Chinese sausage, use salami instead.*

*To open scallops, use a shuck knife. Put the scallop shell on a towel, and hold it down with another towel. Insert the shuck knife into the scallop shell. Turn the shuck knife 90 degrees and the scallop will open.*

I remember going into a Chinese supermarket with my mother and asking her why the sausages looked so funny. She explained that they were *lap cheong* (臘腸) sausages, a Chinese specialty usually made from pork with a high fat content, which are normally smoked, sweetened, and seasoned with rose water, rice wine, and soy sauce. She bought a couple and promised to make me surf and turf when we got home, which sounded very exciting. I remember watching as she heated up the wok, how it crackled with bright red flickers of fire, and how I covered my ears as she added the oil. Then she skillfully used her chopsticks to position each scallop in the wok before adding the sliced *lap cheong*. The smells were sensational and the taste was equally delicious.

METHOD

Heat a wok over high heat and add the oil. Add the sliced sausage and cook for 2 minutes, stirring until crisp. Remove from the wok and set aside.

Return the wok to high heat, put in the scallops, and sear them for 2–3 minutes on each side—or until they are nicely brown on both sides. Season with salt. Add the scallions, return the Chinese sausage to the pan, and stir-fry for 1 minute.

# CELEBRATION LOBSTER NOODLES
# 龍蝦伊面

*Use gluten-free noodles (see page 156). Use tamari rather than oyster sauce and soy sauce.*

*Dairy free*

*Serves 2*

*Preparation time 20 minutes*

*Cooking time 30 minutes*

**2 live lobsters, each one weighing approx. 2½ lbs**

**14oz *yee mein* or egg noodles**

**3 tablespoons vegetable oil**

**2-inch piece of fresh ginger, peeled and finely chopped**

**3 scallions, cut into 1-inch lengths**

**2 teaspoons salt**

**2 teaspoons sugar**

*For the sauce*

**2 tablespoons light soy sauce**

**4 tablespoons oyster sauce**

**freshly ground black pepper**

**2 teaspoons sugar**

**1 teaspoon sesame oil**

**2 tablespoons Shaoxing rice wine**

**½ cup water**

**\*Lisa's tips**

*This dish is fit for a king! The ginger and scallions complement the lobster perfectly.*

When we set up Sweet Mandarin in 2004, aged twenty-something, we struggled to get a mortgage with the banks. Determined to turn our dream into a reality, we decided to sell our houses, plough the money into our restaurant, and move back in with our parents. We bought a plot of land in the northern quarter of Manchester and, against this equity, borrowed to build Sweet Mandarin. At the restaurant's launch party, we served this dish with Champagne. It had been a challenge to get our venture off the ground, but it was a huge achievement worthy of such a luxurious dish.

METHOD

Put the first lobster on a sturdy chopping board. Take a sharp, heavy chopping knife and align the point on the central line about an inch behind the eyes. Holding the lobster steady, quickly bring the knife down through the head of the lobster to completely dissect the head in two lengthwise. Immediately turn the lobster around and cut the lobster in half lengthwise, from head to tail. Clean out the green stomach/intestinal tract thoroughly, remove the claws and chop the tail into 2-inch pieces. Lightly crack the lobster claws with a hammer, keeping them intact. Blot the pieces of lobster dry with paper towels and set aside in a bowl. Scrape any of the juices from the chopping board into a bowl and set aside to add to the sauce later. Repeat with the second lobster.

Fill a large saucepan with cold water and bring to a boil. Add the noodles and cook for 5 minutes; drain in a colander and refresh under cold water.

Heat a large wok over high heat until very hot. Add 2 tablespoons of oil, throw in the ginger and scallions, and cook for 1 minute, stirring, to release their fragrance. Add the lobster parts and stir-fry for 15–20 minutes or until they turn a vivid red color all over.

Add the ingredients for the sauce, along with any of the lobster juices, and bring to a boil. Remove from the heat and set aside.

To reheat the noodles, heat a separate wok over high heat and add 1 tablespoon of oil. Add the cooked noodles and stir-fry briefly until heated through. Season with salt and sugar.

To serve, pile the noodles on a serving dish and spoon over the lobster and sauce.

# STEAMED MUSSELS IN CHINESE RICE WINE

## 米酒蒸帶子

*Gluten free*

*Dairy free*

*Egg free*

Serves 2

Preparation time 15 minutes

Cooking time 10 minutes

**1 tablespoon vegetable oil**

**3 garlic cloves, very finely chopped**

**2 shallots, very finely chopped**

**1 chile, seeded and very finely chopped**

**1 lb mussels (preferably live), scrubbed with beards removed**

**¼ cup Shaoxing rice wine**

**¼ cup water**

**a handful of cilantro leaves, roughly chopped**

**\*Lisa's tips**

*Use live mussels for ultimate freshness and flavor. To prepare, wash them carefully in several changes of water and tap each one gently to make sure it is still alive. If they are fresh, the mussels should close when you tap them; any that remain open are dead and should be discarded. You should also throw away any mussels that don't open once cooked.*

Mussels are a natural aphrodisiac and we often serve them at Sweet Mandarin for special occasions such as Valentine's Day. Here is a real life Valentine's story I experienced one evening that touched my heart and has been recorded in my memory ever since.

One night a handsome young man came to Sweet Mandarin armed with a CD and an ancient scroll. He'd come to inspect the table, table 3 in the alcove, and also to check his order of live mussels. He told me how he had first struck up a conversation with his girlfriend at that table three years ago when he coaxed her into tasting a bowl of mussels. She had initially been wary about trying them, but it was their shared love for mussels on that night that eventually brought them together.

Tonight he was going to propose to that very same girl, whom he had first met at Sweet Mandarin, and he wanted everything to be just perfect. He had planned out the evening carefully—every course, the music and all the fine details—and when the couple finally sat down it was so tense you could hear a pin drop. He gave me the nod and I delivered the mussels, along with the scroll outlining his feelings. As his girlfriend started to read the poignant words, she cried tears of joy and my eyes welled up as I witnessed her acceptance. Since then, whenever I cook this simple, meaningful dish I think about that precious moment at Sweet Mandarin and how we helped that couple's dreams come true.

METHOD

Heat a wok over high heat and add the oil. Stir-fry the garlic, shallots, and chile together for 1 minute to release their aroma into the oil. Throw in the mussels, add the wine and water, and toss gently to mix. Cover the wok with a lid and bubble away vigorously for 5 minutes or until all the shells have opened. Discard any shells that remain closed. Sprinkle with the chopped cilantro and serve.

# SQUID WITH BLACK BEANS
## 豆豉炒鮮魷

*Gluten free*

*Dairy free*

*Egg free*

*Serves 2*

*Preparation time 15 minutes*

*Cooking time 15 minutes*

**8oz raw squid tubes**

**2 tablespoons vegetable oil**

**3 garlic cloves, finely sliced**

**2 tablespoons fermented black beans**

**1 small cucumber, cut into thin**
    **slices on the diagonal**

**2 scallions, finely sliced**

**¼ cup chicken or vegetable stock**

*(see pages 12–13)*

**1 teaspoon salt**

**1 teaspoon sugar**

**2 tablespoons potato starch mixture**

*(see page 8)*

**½ teaspoon sesame oil**

**\*Lisa's tips**

*Avoid overseasoning the squid as this*
*dish is already salty from the fermented*
*black beans.*

For this recipe, when I say black beans I'm referring to salted black beans—soy beans that have been fermented with salt and partially dried to enhance their flavor. These are not the black beans you'll find in Latin American dishes.

METHOD

First prepare the squid tubes. Cut each tube down one side and open out flat. Score the flesh with diagonal lines, first one way and then the other, to create a lattice pattern all over. Cut the squid into 2-inch pieces and set aside.

Heat a wok over high heat and add the oil. Stir-fry the garlic and black beans for 1 minute to release their fragrance into the oil. Add the pieces of squid, which will curl immediately, and stir-fry for 3 minutes.

Add the cucumber and scallions and stir-fry for 2 minutes. Pour in the stock, season with salt and sugar, and cook for another 5 minutes. Add the potato starch mixture and stir vigorously to thicken the sauce. Drizzle with the sesame oil and serve immediately.

It is very easy to overlook the vegetable dishes in a cookbook. However, in China vegetables are classed as the unsung heroes of the meal.

Back in the 1960s, the only place our grandmother could buy Chinese vegetables and rice was in Liverpool, but the only way Lily could get there was by car. In those days, not many people had cars so Lily decided to buy herself a secondhand one. Negotiations with the garage were simple for Lily, who based her choice purely on color: "I'll take the red one," she said, "that looks lucky." And that was the end of it. Luckily for Lily, the car was half decent and off she drove every Sunday to Liverpool Docks to stock up. The only problem was that Lily was a bad driver—one time she was caught by a policeman going around a traffic circle the wrong way—but that didn't matter. He recognized our grandmother immediately and let her off, saying he thought her food was delicious and admitting that whenever he took a take-out home to his wife, he was always in her good books. These vegetables remind me of that story. Today we are very lucky to have such an array of vegetables, but back in the 1960s choy sum would have been a real novelty.

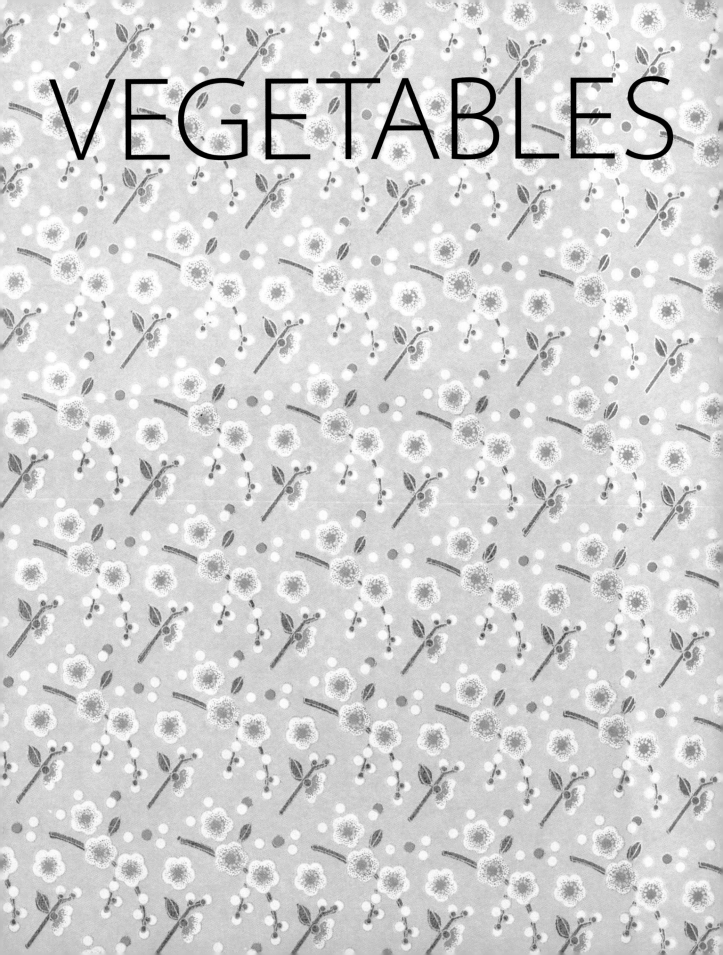

# VEGETABLES

# LIVERPOOL DOCK'S STIR-FRIED CHINESE CHOY SUM
## 蒜蓉炒菜心

Choy sum is really easy to cook and high in vitamin A, vitamin C, vitamin B6, potassium, beta-carotene, calcium, folic acid, and dietary fiber. The simple blanching technique helps to soften the stalks, but retains the freshness.

- *Use tamari rather than soy sauce.*
- *Dairy free*
- *Egg free*

*Serves 2*
*Preparation time 5 minutes*
*Cooking time 15 minutes*

5oz choy sum

1 tablespoon vegetable oil

2 garlic cloves, finely sliced

1 teaspoon salt

1 teaspoon sugar

1 teaspoon light soy sauce

1 teaspoon sesame oil

METHOD

Fill a wok with water and bring to a boil. Add the choy sum and blanch for 5 minutes until just tender. Drain, refresh under cold running water, and set aside.

Heat a wok over high heat and add the oil. Stir-fry the garlic briefly to release its fragrance into the oil, and then add the cooked choy sum. Stir-fry together for 5 minutes before seasoning the dish with salt, sugar, soy sauce, and sesame oil.

Remove the choy sum from the wok and use chopsticks to arrange it on a serving platter so that all the leaves point in the same direction to create a beautiful dish.

# SAUTÉED SQUEAKY STRING BEANS WITH GARLIC AND CHILE
## 椒絲蒜蓉炒四季豆

These funny Chinese beans are known as string beans, snap beans, or even squeaky beans because of the sound they make on your teeth when you chew them. In this recipe, they absorb the flavors of the chile and garlic like a sponge, tantalizing your tastebuds.

- *Gluten free*
- *Dairy free*
- *Egg free*

*Serves 2*
*Preparation time 5 minutes*
*Cooking time 10 minutes*

10oz Chinese string beans, ends trimmed and cut into 3-inch pieces

1 tablespoon vegetable oil

2 garlic cloves, finely sliced

1 fresh red chile, finely sliced

½ teaspoon salt

½ teaspoon sugar

2 tablespoons Shaoxing rice wine

METHOD

Fill a wok with water and bring to a boil. Add the string beans, and blanch for 5 minutes. Drain, refresh under cold running water, and set aside.

Heat a wok over high heat and add the oil. Put in the garlic and chile and stir-fry for 1 minute to release their flavor into the oil. Add the cooked string beans, season with salt, sugar, and Shaoxing wine and stir through until piping hot.

*Lisa's tips

*String beans can sometimes grow yards long and are packed with antioxidants. If you can't get hold of them, use French beans.*

# STIR-FRIED MIXED MUSHROOMS
# 素炒蘑菇

*Gluten free*

*Dairy free*

*Egg free*

*Serves 2*

*Preparation time 15 minutes*

*Cooking time 10 minutes*

**1 tablespoon vegetable oil**

**1-inch piece of fresh ginger,**
**peeled and finely sliced**

**1 teaspoon minced garlic**

**1 scallion, cut into 1-inch lengths**

**6–8 dried Chinese mushrooms,**
**soaked in boiling water for**
**15 minutes then drained and**
**cut in half**

**¾ cup straw mushrooms (kept whole)**

**¾ cup button mushrooms, halved**

**¾ cup oyster mushrooms, halved**

**¾ cup sugar snap peas, finely sliced**

**¾ cup, baby corn, cut in half**
**lengthwise**

**4 tablespoons water**

**1 teaspoon salt**

**1 teaspoon sugar**

**1 teaspoon Shaoxing rice wine**

**\*Lisa's tips**

*This is a feast for vegans and vegetarians.*

As we stepped into the house where our grandmother was born, we saw on the wall a black-and-white photo, which had weathered in the sun. The resemblance of the lady in the photo to our grandmother was startling. It was our grandmother's mother! The man in the photo was our grandmother's father, who looked like our mother with high cheekbones and beautiful eyes. The bridge in the village still stood, but the lake where the fish used to swim had dried up years ago. We went to the temple, a Chinese tradition, to light incense for our ancestors as a sign of respect. In the temple, a very frail elderly lady no taller than 4 feet came out and clasped Lily's hands with tears in her eyes. It was Lily's youngest sister, Mui. Our grandmother had not seen her sister for over forty years.

Later in the day, we sat down with Mui to enjoy a delicious vegetarian dish of mixed mushrooms with sugar snap peas from Mui's nursery and baby corn and scallions from her balcony. Cooking on a wok that must have been twice her size, Mui first fried the garlic and then tossed in the vegetables. Holding the wok with two hands, she deftly poured the delicious medley of vegetables into a bowl with accuracy borne from years of experience. Together, over that simple dish, we celebrated life that day.

METHOD

Heat a wok over high heat and add the oil. Stir-fry the holy trinity of Chinese ingredients—the ginger, garlic, and scallion—for 1 minute in the hot oil to release their aroma. Add all the different types of mushroom, along with the sugar snap peas, corn, and water and toss for 5–7 minutes. Season with salt, sugar, and Shaoxing wine.

# MAPO TOFU
## 麻婆豆腐

🌾 *Use gluten-free chile sauce rather than chile bean paste.*

♥ *Dairy free*

◯ *Egg free*

*Serves 2*

*Preparation time 10 minutes*

*Cooking time 15 minutes*

**1 tablespoon vegetable oil**

**½-inch piece of fresh ginger,
    peeled and sliced**

**7oz ground pork**

**1 teaspoon chile bean sauce**

**1 cup chicken stock** *(see page 12)*

**5oz firm tofu, cut into 1-inch cubes**

**1 teaspoon salt**

**1 teaspoon sugar**

**½ teaspoon Shaoxing rice wine**

**½ teaspoon sesame oil**

**1 scallion, finely chopped,
    to garnish**

***Lisa's tips**

*Add chile oil if you want to make this dish hotter—the tofu will really absorb the flavor of the chile to pack a punch.*

Many people say tofu is bland, rubbery, and unappealing, but on the positive side, it is exceptionally nutritious. In this recipe, I have combined it with pork and chiles to appeal to a wider audience, making this a good introduction to tofu if you have never tasted it before. The word *mapo* is used to describe a person disfigured by smallpox. The story behind this tofu dish is that it was named after a pock-marked old lady from Szechuan, who was also a skillful cook.

METHOD

Heat a wok on high heat and add the oil. Put in the ginger and pork and stir-fry continuously over high heat until the pork is almost cooked. This takes approx. 10 minutes.

Add the chile bean sauce and stir well to combine. Pour in the chicken stock and stir again. Nestle the pieces of tofu in the sauce and carefully spoon some of the sauce over the top to keep them moist; don't overmix the dish at this stage or you will break up the tofu. Season with salt, sugar, Shaoxing wine, and sesame oil. Reduce the heat to low and simmer gently for 2 minutes until the sauce has reduced by half.

To serve, spoon the tofu and sauce into a deep bowl, garnish with the scallion, and accompany with jasmine rice.

# CHINESE BROCCOLI (KAI LAN) WITH OYSTER SAUCE
## 蠔油芥蘭

Kai lan looks nothing like broccoli, nor does it taste like broccoli, but it has inherited the name Chinese broccoli. It tastes sweet and fresh and should make you smile when you bite into it because it's really, really good for you.

- *Use tamari rather than oyster sauce.*
- *Dairy free*
- *Egg free*
- *Serves 2*
- *Preparation time 5 minutes*
- *Cooking time 10 minutes*

**7oz Chinese broccoli (kai lan)**
**2 tablespoons oyster sauce**

METHOD
Separate the Chinese broccoli stems and wash in cold water. Shake off any excess water.

Fill a wok with water and bring to a boil. Add the Chinese broccoli and blanch for 5–7 minutes until just cooked through; drain.

To serve, arrange the cooked kai lan on a serving plate and drizzle some oyster sauce over the top—simple, yet delightful.

**\*Lisa's tips**
*Don't overboil the kai lan or it will become soggy.*

# STIR-FRIED BOK CHOY
*(Krystal's favorite)*
## 炒白菜

One downside to a job that requires daily manual labor is that my body aches after the weekend service. To keep supple, I have a massage: I always go to the same person, Krystal. She's an absolute lifesaver and has even used crystals to rejuvenate me. In return, she asks me to make this dish for her.

- *Use tamari rather than soy sauce.*
- *Dairy free*
- *Egg free*
- *Serves 2*
- *Preparation time 5 minutes*
- *Cooking time 10 minutes*

**10 stems of bok choy, root end trimmed**
**½ tablespoon vegetable oil**
**3 garlic cloves, finely chopped**
**½ teaspoon salt**
**½ teaspoon sugar**
**½ teaspoon sesame oil**
**½ teaspoon light soy sauce**

METHOD
Separate the bok choy leaves and rinse well.

Fill a wok with water and bring to a boil. Add the bok choy and blanch for 3–4 minutes. Drain, refresh under cold running water, and set aside.

Dry the wok with paper towels and add the vegetable oil. Add the garlic, stir briefly to release its aroma into the oil, and then add the bok choy. Stir-fry for 4 minutes. Season with salt, sugar, sesame oil, and soy sauce, tossing well to combine.

**\*Lisa's tips**
*Don't overcook the bok choy; the thin leaves wilt very quickly.*

# FRIED TOFU WITH SWEET AND SOUR SAUCE

## 酸甜炸豆腐

*Gluten free*

*Dairy free*

*Egg free*

*Serves 2*

*Preparation time 10 minutes*

*Cooking time 20 minutes*

**vegetable oil, for deep-frying**

**7oz tofu, cut into 1-inch cubes**

**1 onion, finely chopped**

**½ green pepper, cut into small dice**

**½ red pepper, cut into small dice**

**3 pineapple rings, cut into**
   **½-inch chunks**

**1¼ cups sweet and sour sauce**

   *(see page 14)*

**\*Lisa's tips**

*This is a tasty vegetarian/vegan dish.*

Tofu, also called beancurd, is a food made by coagulating soy juice and then pressing the resulting curds into soft white blocks. It is a component of many East Asian and Southeast Asian cuisines. There are many different varieties, including fresh tofu and tofu that has been processed in some way. Tofu has a subtle flavor and so it can be used successfully in savory and sweet dishes. Tofu has a low calorie count, relatively large amounts of protein, and little fat. It is high in iron and, depending on the coagulant used in manufacturing, may also be high in calcium and/or magnesium. Tofu in its natural form is soft, but in this recipe it is fried to harden it up—the result is a crispy texture that contrasts beautifully with the tangy sweet and sour sauce.

METHOD

Fill a wok with approx. $^1/_3$ cup vegetable oil and preheat over medium heat to 350°F. Test the temperature using a bamboo chopstick (see page 35). Lower the tofu cubes into the hot oil—they should sizzle immediately—and deep-fry for 5–7 minutes until golden brown. Remove the tofu with a slotted spoon and drain on paper towels. Meanwhile, carefully pour the oil from the wok into a metal container, keeping approx. 1 tablespoon of oil in the pan.

Return the wok to high heat and cook the onion, peppers, and pineapple until they start to soften, approx. 2 minutes. Pour in the sweet and sour sauce and bring to a boil. Nestle the pieces of crispy tofu in the sauce and toss well to combine.

# EGGPLANT CASSEROLE
# 茄子煲

*Serves 2*

*Preparation time 10 minutes*

*Cooking time 20 minutes*

**2 large eggplants, cut into**
   **3-inch wedges**

**3 tablespoons vegetable oil**

**3 garlic cloves, finely sliced**

**7oz ground pork**

**2 scallions, finely sliced**

**¼ cup chicken stock** *(see page 12)*

**½ teaspoon salt**

**½ teaspoon sugar**

**½ teaspoon sesame oil**

**2 tablespoons potato starch mixture**
   *(see page 8)*

**\*Lisa's tips**
*You can use either black or purple eggplants for this dish; cooked this way they both taste equally delicious. Ensure the skin of the eggplant is shiny and smooth—if it is wrinkly, then it is old and will not taste as fresh.*

Eggplant can be a tricky ingredient to cook and often ends up greasy if you use too much oil. A good tip is to blanch the eggplant slices briefly to soften them before frying—that way, they require less time to cook and don't need so much oil when you come to fry them. Blanching should also eliminate the slight bitter taste sometimes associated with eggplants.

METHOD
Bring a saucepan of water to a boil, add the eggplant, and cook for 4 minutes. Drain thoroughly and pat dry on paper towels.

Heat a wok over high heat and add the oil. Add the garlic and stir briefly to release the flavor into the oil. Add the pork and fry for 10 minutes, stirring continuously, until cooked through.

Add the cooked eggplant, scallions and stock, and mix well together. Bring to a boil and cook for 3 minutes. Season with salt, sugar, and sesame oil, and then add the potato starch mixture and stir vigorously to thicken the sauce. Serve with jasmine rice.

# GREEN CURRY WITH VEGETABLES
綠咖哩雜菜

*Gluten free*

*Dairy free*

*Egg free*

*Serves 2*

*Preparation time 15 minutes*

*Cooking time 15 minutes*

1 tablespoon vegetable oil

1 x 14oz can of coconut milk

1 medium onion, roughly chopped

4oz bamboo shoots

4oz water chestnuts

1½ cups Napa cabbage, cut into
bite-sized pieces

1 carrot, peeled and cut into thin
slices on the diagonal

1 eggplant, cut into 1-inch cubes

1 cup chicken stock *(see page 12)*

¼ cup grated coconut (optional)

½ teaspoon salt

1 teaspoon sugar

juice of ½ lime

*For the green curry paste*

3 green bird's eye chiles

2 stalks of lemongrass, chopped

6 scallions, chopped

1 tablespoon minced ginger

1 tablespoon ground coriander

3 garlic cloves, chopped

¼ teaspoon shrimp paste

½ teaspoon salt

2 teaspoons brown sugar

juice of 1 lime, plus 1 teaspoon
lime zest

2–3 tablespoons vegetable oil

½ teaspoon white pepper

Our grandmother came to the UK in the 1950s. The ship took 35 days to sail from Hong Kong to Liverpool, taking in Singapore, Penang, Ceylon, Bombay, the Suez Canal, Gibraltar, and Southampton along the way. It was on this journey that Lily perfected her green curry recipe, which wooed the local community in Manchester on her arrival. Elements of the dish were learned in Singapore, where Lily stopped off to visit her sister (who had relocated there with her husband) and the secret blend of spices was perfected in Bombay.

Today green curry is a firm favorite of the family, especially on cold days when the heat of the dish helps to warm you up. Any leftover curry paste can be spooned into a jar and stored in the fridge for up to 2 weeks. If you don't have time to make your own green curry paste, use ½ tablespoon of store-bought paste instead.

METHOD

Prepare the curry paste by mixing together all of the ingredients in a blender. Blend to a smooth paste.

Heat the oil in a wok over high heat and fry ½ tablespoon of the green curry paste to release its fragrance into the oil, approx. 1 minute. Add the coconut milk, stirring well to blend.

Bring to a boil, throw in all the vegetables, and simmer gently for 5 minutes. Add the chicken stock, and boil until the sauce has reduced by one-third, which takes approx. 5 minutes.

Stir in the grated coconut (if using) and season with salt, sugar, and lime juice. Serve with fragrant steamed rice.

Just like the 1.3 billion Chinese people living in China, our mother believes that noodles represent longevity and should therefore never be cut—otherwise you cut short your own life. While life might have been tough for Mabel, growing up in the only Chinese family in Middleton, and the only Chinese girl at school, she was determined to have a long life—so she never cut her noodles!

Rice is the staple diet of the Chinese and the customary greeting is "Have you eaten rice yet?" rather than "How are you?" Our grandmother always said that we had to finish our rice, or the man we'd marry would be spotty. She also told us that rice represented a victory for the nation and that every grain was precious, even more so than gold—because gold could not be eaten.

Our grandmother, Lily Kwok, was born in 1918 in south China (Guangzhou) as China tried to recover from World War I and an immense loss of life. The influenza epidemic in 1918–1919 had killed more people than the World War (over 20 million) and piles of corpses lay scattered across the vast plains. Yet our grandmother survived, in spite of this. In China, the rural class was at the whim of bad harvests, famine, and shortages of rice. Her mother sacrificed her bowl of rice so that our grandmother could eat. I'm thankful that my life is not as traumatic as that, but merely extends to ensuring the rice is properly cooked.

麵條和大米

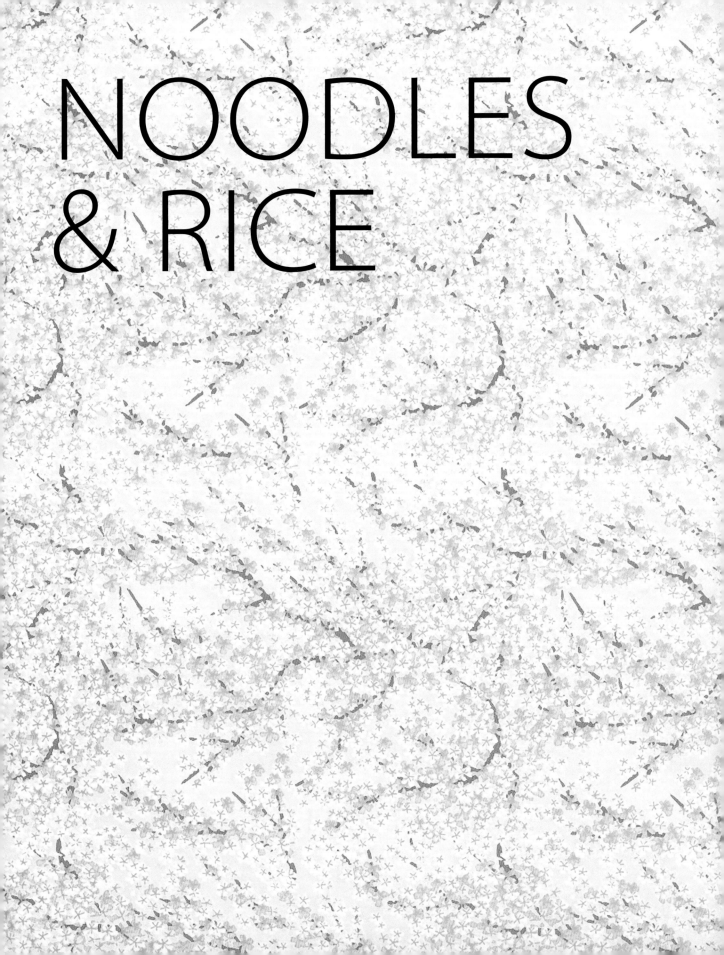

# NOODLES
# & RICE

# SINGAPORE-STYLE RICE VERMICELLI
# 星洲炒米

*Check that the curry paste is gluten free.*

*Dairy free*

*Serves 2*

*Preparation time 15 minutes*

*Cooking time 15 minutes*

2 x 4oz rice vermicelli noodle cakes

2 tablespoons vegetable oil

1 egg, beaten

4oz (1 cup) bean sprouts

1 medium onion, finely sliced

1 medium green pepper, finely sliced

1½ cups (8oz) cooked char siu pork
   *(see page 89)* **or cooked ham,**
   **sliced into strips**

4oz small, cooked, peeled shrimp

1 teaspoon salt

1 teaspoon sugar

1 teaspoon Chinese-style curry paste

1 teaspoon sesame oil

1 teaspoon toasted sesame seeds

**\*Lisa's tips**

*If you don't like the curry flavor, you can omit this and use sweet and sour sauce instead; this gives a totally different taste and is a firm favorite with the kids.*

This is the dish we use to test all our chefs before we hire them. It is quite a difficult dish to master, as there are several cooking techniques involved. However, I have taught this successfully at our cooking school, and my students have managed to replicate this dish at home. The trick is to thin the curry paste with a little water before adding it to the noodles so that it coats them evenly and doesn't clump together.

METHOD

Heat some water in a wok and bring to a boil. Remove the pan from the heat, drop in the noodles, and leave to soak for 5 minutes until soft. Drain the noodles through a colander and refresh under cold running water. Set aside.

Heat a wok over high heat and add the oil. Once the wok is hot, add the beaten egg and mix with a spatula until it scrambles, approx. 2–3 minutes. Add the bean sprouts, onion, pepper, char siu pork (or ham), and shrimp, and mix quickly to combine. Season with a pinch of salt and sugar.

Add the cooked noodles to the pan and stir-fry for 5 minutes. Meanwhile, combine the curry paste in a small bowl with 1 tablespoon of water and mix to a thin paste.

Pour the curry mixture evenly over the noodles, and season with the remaining salt and sugar and the sesame oil. Use your spatula to mix the ingredients together, tossing the wok gently at the same time to stop the noodles from sticking. Continue mixing and tossing until the noodles change color from dark yellow to light yellow, which means the curry paste has cooked through. Sprinkle over the toasted sesame seeds and serve.

# CHICKEN CHOW MEIN
## 雞絲炒麵

Use rice noodles or gluten-free noodles
(see page 156).
Use tamari rather than soy sauce.

Dairy free
Serves 2
Preparation time 15 minutes
Cooking time 30 minutes

**For the chicken**

**7oz boneless chicken breasts,
    thinly sliced**

**1 teaspoon salt**

**1 teaspoon sugar**

**2 tablespoons potato starch mixture**
    (see page 8)

**For the noodles**

**7oz medium dried egg
    noodles or rice noodles**

**2 tablespoons vegetable oil**

**½ cup bean sprouts**

**2 teaspoons light soy sauce**

**For the topping**

**2 tablespoons vegetable oil**

**½-inch piece of fresh ginger,
    peeled and thinly sliced**

**¾ cup (2oz) snow peas**

**1 medium onion, finely sliced**

**5 tablespoons vegetable stock**
    (see page 13)

**1 teaspoon salt**

**1 teaspoon sugar**

**1 teaspoon sesame oil**

**2 teaspoons light soy sauce**

**1 teaspoon Shaoxing rice wine**

**2 tablespoons potato starch mixture**
    (see page 8)

When our grandmother and mother set up our restaurant in Middleton, the locals had never tasted Chinese food before and, initially, they were skeptical. Back in the 1950s, Spaghetti Bolognese was as foreign as Chicken Chow Mein—and yet in time both delighted the local palate. When they started the restaurant, Lily and Mabel (together with our uncle) were the targets for thieves and troublemakers, but after a while their tempting dishes started to woo the residents and business soon picked up. Chicken Chow Mein became the talk of the town—in fact, our grandmother and mother were probably instrumental in making it one of the nation's favorites.

Traditionally, Chicken Chow Mein would have been made with a mixture of odds and ends of vegetables from the store, paired with soft, chewy noodles. Feel free to adjust the vegetables in the recipe, according to what you have available.

METHOD

Combine the chicken in a bowl with the salt, sugar, and potato starch mixture and set aside to marinate in the fridge for at least 10 minutes. Soak the dried noodles in a bowl of boiling water until they have softened, approx. 4–5 minutes. Tip them into a colander, refresh under cold running water, and set aside to drain.

Bring a pan of water to a boil, add the chicken pieces and blanch for 10 minutes until fully cooked. Drain and refresh under cold running water.

Heat 2 tablespoons of oil in a hot wok. Add the bean sprouts and the noodles and stir-fry for 3 minutes. Season with a pinch of salt and sugar and the soy sauce. Cook for another 5–7 minutes, tossing constantly. Tip the noodles onto a large serving platter and cover loosely with foil to keep them warm.

To make the topping, return the same wok to high heat and add 2 tablespoons of oil. Put in the ginger, snow peas, and onion and stir-fry for 1 minute. Add the cooked chicken and stock and continue to stir-fry for another 5 minutes until the vegetables are cooked through. Season with salt, sugar, sesame oil, soy sauce and Shaoxing wine, tossing well to combine. Bring the sauce to a boil and add the potato starch mixture, stirring vigorously to thicken.

To serve, pour the chicken stir-fry mixture over the noodles.

# QUICK AND EASY STIR-FRIED NOODLES
## 炒麵

Use tamari rather than soy sauce. Use rice noodles or gluten-free noodles (see page 156).

Dairy free

Serves 2

Preparation time 5 minutes

Cooking time 15 minutes

**7oz medium dried egg noodles**

**1 tablespoon vegetable oil**

**3oz (¾ cup) bean sprouts**

**1–2 scallions, cut into**
**    1-inch lengths**

**1 teaspoon salt**

**1 teaspoon sugar**

**1 teaspoon light soy sauce**

**\*Lisa's tips**

*The bean sprouts are a helpful addition because they stop the noodles from sticking to the wok.*

This simple recipe makes a great noodle side dish.

METHOD

Fill a wok with water and bring to a boil. Remove the wok from the heat, drop in the noodles, and leave to soak for 5 minutes until soft. Drain in a colander, refresh under cold running water, and set aside.

Dry the wok with paper towels, put over high heat, and add the oil. Add the bean sprouts and scallions and stir-fry for 1 minute. Tip in the cooked noodles and, using the edge of the spatula, toss them around in the pan so that they separate. Season with salt, sugar, and soy sauce. Continue to cook for another 10 minutes, tossing gently to keep the noodles moving so that they don't stick to the bottom of the pan.

# SZECHUAN-STYLE COLD CHICKEN SOBA NOODLES WITH SPINACH
## 四川雞柳配蕎麥麵

*Gluten free*

*Dairy free*

Serves 2

*Preparation time 30 minutes*

*Cooking time 10 minutes*

*For the gluten-free soba noodles*

¾ **cup buckwheat flour**

½ **cup tapioca flour**

1 **teaspoon garlic powder**

2 **eggs**

3 **teaspoons xanthan gum**

1 **teaspoon salt**

2 **tablespoons vegetable oil**

2 **tablespoons cooled boiled water**

*For the chicken*

2 **tablespoons vegetable oil**

7oz **boneless chicken breast, cut into thin strips**

2 **teaspoons salt**

2 **teaspoons sugar**

3 **cups spinach, washed thoroughly**

*For the Szechuan salad dressing*

1 **tablespoon white wine vinegar**

1 **teaspoon sugar**

½ **teaspoon salt**

½ **teaspoon chile oil**

¼ **teaspoon sesame oil**

¼ **teaspoon ground black pepper**

**∗Lisa's tips**

*Despite its name, buckwheat is not made of wheat but is related to rhubarb and has a slightly nutty flavor.*

Szechuan province is renowned for its chiles and boasts that "China is the place for food, Szechuan is the place for flavor." I remember enjoying these wonderful noodles during a visit to Szechuan. Against a backdrop of breathtaking mountains, which reminded me of a Chinese calligraphy painting, I sat by a vast river watching the fishing boats bob on the water, intoxicated by the fragrance of the chiles. Szechuans believe that chiles are the heart of the nation and that if you can't take the heat, you aren't a real Szechuan. It is certainly true that Szechuan peppercorns and red chiles create that biting, numbing, spicy hotness that many people revel in. In this dish they are tempered with cooling noodles, which offer a refreshing bite before the chiles kick in.

METHOD

To make the noodles, combine all the ingredients in a food processor and process for 3 minutes until the mixture comes together in a ball. Roll out the dough using a pasta machine or a rolling pin to a thickness of about a tenth of an inch and cut into thin strips.

Half-fill a wok with water and bring to a boil. Remove the wok from the heat, drop in the noodles, and set aside to soak for 3 minutes. Tip the noodles into a colander, refresh under cold running water to halt the cooking process, and set aside to drain.

Add the oil to a preheated wok and stir-fry the chicken for 10 minutes over high heat with the salt and sugar. Set aside to cool.

Blanch the spinach leaves in boiling water for 30 seconds, and then drain in a colander and refresh under cold running water.

To make the Szechuan dressing, combine all the ingredients in a small bowl and whisk together.

To serve, combine the noodles, chicken, and spinach in a salad bowl, pour on the dressing, and toss well to combine.

# WONTON DUMPLING NOODLE SOUP

## 雲吞湯麵

*Serves 2 (as a main course)*
*Preparation time 10 minutes*
*Cooking time 15 minutes*

**7oz medium dried egg noodles**
**20 wonton dumplings** (see page 20)
**2 cups chicken stock** (see page 12)
**½ teaspoon salt**
**½ teaspoon sugar**
**1 teaspoon light soy sauce**
**½ teaspoon sesame oil**
**1 scallion, finely sliced**
**6 bok choy leaves, separated**

**\*Lisa's tips**
*Wontons can be made in advance and frozen for up to a month until needed, making this a quick and easy dish to have on standby.*

For this recipe, I have bulked up the wonton soup dish on page 20 with some noodles to make it suitable for a main course. This dish is perfect when you are feeling cold or under the weather and need a pick-me-up.

METHOD
Half fill a wok with water and bring to a boil. Remove the pan from the heat, drop in the dried noodles, and set aside to soak for 5 minutes. Once they have softened, tip the noodles into a colander and refresh under cold running water. Portion out the noodles into two soup bowls.

Refill the wok with water and bring to a boil. Drop the wontons into the wok, bring the water back to a boil, and cook for 5 minutes. Drain through a colander and divide between the two soup bowls, placing the wontons on top of the cooked noodles. Rinse out the wok and dry thoroughly.

Heat the chicken stock in the wok and season with salt, sugar, soy sauce, and sesame oil. Bring to a boil, add the chopped scallion and whole bok choy leaves, and simmer for 5 minutes. To serve, pour the hot broth over the noodles and wontons.

# CRISPY SHRIMP TEMPURA WITH MISO SOUP UDON
## 大蝦天婦羅湯烏冬

❤ *Dairy free*

⊖ *Egg free*

*Serves 2*

*Preparation time 15 minutes*

*Cooking time 20 minutes*

**7oz jumbo shrimp,**
   **peeled and deveined**

**1 teaspoon salt**

*For the noodles*

**7oz thick udon noodles**

**2 cups chicken stock** *(see page 12)*

**1 carrot, peeled and finely sliced**
   **into rounds**

**1½ cups (5oz) snow peas**

**2 tablespoons corn**

**2 tablespoons white miso paste**

**1 scallion, finely sliced**

*For the tempura batter*

**¾ cup self-rising flour**

**6 ice cubes**

**⅔ cup seltzer**

**vegetable oil, for deep-frying**

✳**Lisa's tips**

*Japanese tempura shrimp are a real treat, but the batter can be hard to get right. The trick is to ensure that the batter is ice cold and lumpy so that it pops when it goes into the hot oil, resulting in a light batter with little, airy craters.*

Our grandmother once surprised me when she started speaking Japanese to the fishmonger while ordering her shrimp. She picked up the language during the Japanese occupation of Hong Kong during World War II and felt that the Japanese language and food were great positives she was able to take from an unpleasant experience.

METHOD

Fill a medium saucepan with water and bring to a boil. Remove from the heat, drop in the noodles, and set aside to soak for 5 minutes or until they have softened. Drain the noodles through a colander, refresh under cold running water, and divide them between two serving bowls.

Bring the stock to a boil in a large saucepan. Add the carrots and cook for 3 minutes until tender. Add the snow peas and cook for 1 minute or until they turn bright green. Finally add the corn and cook for 30 seconds. Remove the pan from the heat and set aside.

Scoop the miso into a bowl, add 2 ladlefuls of the hot broth, and whisk thoroughly until the miso has completely dissolved. Pour the miso mixture back into the pan and return to a moderate heat. Do not let the soup boil or the miso will become gritty. Stir in the scallion and pour the broth immediately over the noodles.

To make the tempura batter, put the flour in a mixing bowl. Put in the ice cubes and add the seltzer, little by little, stirring with a wooden spoon until the mixture comes together. The finished batter should be the consistency of lumpy cream.

Half fill a wok with oil and preheat over medium heat. Season the shrimp with salt. Holding them by their tails, dip the shrimp into the tempura batter and allow any excess to drip away. Carefully drop the battered shrimp into the hot oil and deep-fry for 5 minutes—the batter should expand slightly in the hot oil and puff up to create small craters. Remove the shrimp from the hot oil with a slotted spoon and drain on paper towels. Serve with the udon soup.

# XO SAUCE NOODLES
# 醬炒麵

🌾 *Use rice noodles or gluten-free noodles.*

♥ *Dairy free*

◑ *Egg free*

*Serves 2*

*Preparation time 45 minutes*
     *(includes making the XO sauce)*

*Cooking time 20 minutes*

**7oz Shanghai noodles**

**1 tablespoon vegetable oil**

**1–2 slices of bacon, finely diced**

**4oz (1 cup) bean sprouts**

**1 scallion, finely sliced**

*For the XO sauce*

**1oz dried scallops**

**3oz dried shrimp**

**1 cup vegetable oil**

**2 whole garlic heads, cloves**
     **finely chopped**

**½ cup finely diced shallots**

**½-inch piece of fresh ginger,**
     **finely minced**

**3 tablespoons finely sliced fresh long**
     **red chiles**

**3 tablespoons dried long red chiles,**
     **finely sliced**

**2 tablespoons dried red bird's**
     **eye chiles, finely sliced**

**1 teaspoon roasted shrimp paste**
     **(belacan)**

**1 tablespoon brown sugar**

**1 cup water**

**2 tablespoons Shaoxing wine**

**½ teaspoon salt**

Christmas Day 1990, Manchester, UK

"Pass me the XO, Helen," said Dad, and I passed him the cognac, which was covered in dust. "No, not that XO, the other XO." He meant the XO sauce. I was right to be confused.

XO sauce was introduced to Hong Kong during the 1980s. Named after XO (extra old cognac), it was targeted at the upper echelons of society who enjoyed cognac. *Vogue* China once called it the "caviar of the East" and claimed that if there is one thing you should try before you died, it should be this spicy, dried scallop sauce packed with umami flavors.

Today XO is widely available from good Chinese supermarkets, but if you would like to make it yourself, you can follow my recipe. Just make sure you use the very best-quality dried scallops.

METHOD

First make the XO sauce. Put the dried scallops and dried shrimp into separate bowls and pour in enough lukewarm water to cover; set aside to soak for 15 minutes.

Drain the scallops (reserving the soaking liquid) and tear them into fine shreds. Pat dry on paper towels and set aside. Drain the shrimp (reserving the soaking liquid), chop them finely, and set aside.

Heat ½ cup oil in a wok (or large saucepan) over medium-high heat and test the temperature (see page 35). Add the scallops to the hot oil and deep-fry until very crisp, approx. 1–2 minutes. Remove them with a slotted spoon and drain on paper towels. Carefully pour off the hot oil into a heatproof measuring cup and top up with the rest of the oil. Wipe out the wok (or saucepan) with paper towels.

Pour the oil into the wok and set over medium heat. When the oil is hot, add the garlic, shallot, ginger, and soaked chopped shrimp and stir continuously until they turn an even golden brown, approx. 4–5 minutes.

Add the fresh and dried chiles and fry for a few seconds until crisp. Add the shrimp paste, fried scallops, and reserved scallop and shrimp liquid, and stir continuously for a few more seconds. Add the remaining ingredients and continue to cook for another 20–30 minutes, stirring occasionally, until the water has completely evaporated and the sauce is fragrant.

Remove the pan from the heat and carefully strain the oil through a nylon sieve into a clean, heatproof cup. Transfer the solids to a sterilized 1¼ cup canning jar. Carefully pour the hot fragrant oil over the solids to cover. Set aside to cool*.

To make the noodles, fill a medium pan with water and bring to a boil. Remove the pan from the heat, drop in the noodles, and set aside for 5 minutes to soften. Drain through a colander and refresh under cold running water.

Add 1 tablespoon of oil to a preheated wok and stir-fry the bacon until slightly crisp, approx. 4 minutes. Add the bean sprouts and scallion and stir-fry together for 5 minutes. Tip in the cooked noodles, add 1 tablespoon of XO sauce and stir-fry for 5–8 minutes until heated through.

* Once cold, the XO sauce should be stored in a sealed container in the fridge and used within a month.

**\*Lisa's tips**

*If you don't have time to make the XO sauce (or can't get hold of the ingredients), you can buy ready-made XO sauce from good Chinese supermarkets.*

# BEEF HOR FUN NOODLES
# 乾炒牛河

🌾 *Use tamari rather than soy sauce.*

🖤 *Dairy free*

⚪ *Egg free*

*Serves 2*

*Preparation time 15 minutes*

*Cooking time 20 minutes*

**10oz beef tenderloin, thinly sliced**

**1 teaspoon salt**

**1 teaspoon sugar**

**2 tablespoons potato starch**

*For the noodles*

**7oz thick dried rice noodles**
**(also known as hor fun noodles)**

**6 tablespoons vegetable oil**

**1 medium onion, finely sliced**

**7oz (2 cups) bean sprouts**

**3 tablespoons dark soy sauce**

**1 teaspoon salt**

**1 teaspoon sugar**

**1 teaspoon sesame oil**

**\*Lisa's tips**

*Slice the beef finely to ensure it cooks evenly. Rice noodles come in all different sizes—for this dish, I recommend you use noodles that are ½-inch thick to give the dish some texture.*

This used to be one of my favorite dishes when I was a child, and we often used to have it for Sunday lunch. It was also a dish our mother enjoyed eating when she was a child growing up in Hong Kong, as it was popular with the street hawkers. On one occasion, Mabel says her stomach was growling so much as she walked past a street vendor cooking this delicious noodle dish that a passerby gave her a penny to buy a portion!

Life was tough growing up in Hong Kong after World War II. By 1950, the population had surged to an estimated 2.2 million, due to the influx of refugees fleeing violence and political uncertainty in China, and the subsequent lack of housing resulted in 300,000 squatters building tin and board huts on slopes that were too steep for development. Not far from this chaos our family lived, immersing itself in a life of street-cooking, hawker-style. This dish is dedicated to that forgotten world in Hong Kong, which has since been demolished.

METHOD

Combine the beef, salt, sugar, and potato starch in a bowl. Cover with plastic wrap and set aside to marinate for 15 minutes.

Meanwhile, bring some water to a boil in a wok. Remove from the heat, drop in the dried noodles, and set aside to soak for 5 minutes until soft. Tip the noodles into a colander and refresh under cold running water. Set aside.

Heat a wok over high heat and add the vegetable oil. Stir-fry the beef in the hot oil until cooked to your liking, approx. 5–8 minutes. Remove the beef with a slotted spoon and set aside. Drain off the excess oil, leaving a light coating in the pan.

Return the wok to high heat and stir-fry the onion and bean sprouts for 2 minutes until they start to soften. Return the beef to the wok, add the cooked noodles, and toss gently together to stop the noodles from sticking.

Add the soy sauce, salt, sugar, and sesame oil and continue to cook for another 2 minutes, tossing the pan continuously until the noodles are piping hot.

# STEAMED BOILED RICE
## 絲苗飯

Our grandmother taught us a foolproof way of calculating the amount of water needed by measuring using our fingers and knuckles—it works every time.

- *Gluten free*
- *Dairy free*
- *Egg free*

*Serves 2*

*Preparation time 5 minutes*

*Cooking time 20 minutes*

**½ cup long grain white rice**

**⅔ cup cold water**

METHOD

Rinse the rice with cold water and drain. Repeat this process three times or until the water runs clear rather than cloudy; washing the rice removes excess starch and dust.

Tip the rice into a saucepan and add the cold water. Put the pan over high heat and boil the rice for 15 minutes until all of the water has evaporated; there is no need to add salt or oil. If necessary, scrape down the rice around the sides of the pan with a fork to ensure it cooks evenly. Reduce the heat to low for the last 5 minutes. To check the rice is cooked, pinch a few grains between your fingertips—they should feel soft and fluffy.

**\*Lisa's tips**

*Now for our grandmother's special trick to calculate whether you have the perfect amount of water: place your hand in the pan so that the third finger touches the top of the rice and top up the water so it is level with the second knuckle on the third finger. Any leftover rice can be used for Egg-fried Rice (see page 167) .*

# RED RICE
## 紅米飯

Bhutanese red rice is the staple diet of the people of Bhutan. It makes a good alternative to brown rice if you want a change—and cooks faster because it has been semi-milled. Once cooked, the color is pale pink and the texture soft and slightly sticky.

- *Gluten free*
- *Dairy free*
- *Egg free*

*Serves 2*

*Preparation time 5 minutes*

*Cooking time 25 minutes*

**½ cup red rice**

**⅔ cup cold water**

METHOD

Wash the rice with cold water and drain. Repeat this process three times until the water runs clear rather than cloudy.

Tip the rice into a saucepan, add the water, and bring to a boil over high heat. Cover with a lid, reduce the heat to low, and simmer for about 20 minutes until all of the liquid has been absorbed.

Remove the pan from the heat and set aside to stand, still covered with the lid, for 5 minutes before serving.

**\*Lisa's tips**

*Red rice is semi-milled, leaving a thin layer of flaky skin on the grain that contains all the nutrients and fiber.*

# BROWN RICE
## 糙米飯

- Gluten free
- Dairy free
- Egg free

*Serves 2*

*Preparation time 5 minutes*

*Cooking time 50 minutes*

**¼ cup brown rice**

**¼ cup cold water**

**\*Lisa's tips**

*Brown rice is perfect for people with diabetes because it lowers the blood sugar levels.*

*This is the best way to wash rice: fill the container that will be used to cook the rice with cold water and then mix the rice with the cold water. Pour out the water carefully and keep the rice in the container. Do this three times until the water runs clear.*

When our grandmother turned 80 years old, she was diagnosed with diabetes, and the doctor recommended she change her diet from white rice to brown rice. This didn't go down well. The first night I made dinner for her using brown rice, she exclaimed: "Aiy or!"—"Oh no!" in Chinese—"brown rice is the sludge we had during the war and it went right through me."

"No," I reassured her, "It's different now. Brown rice is good for you. It costs even more than white rice."

I turned on the television and we watched an episode of *Friends* together as dinner was cooking. She loved that sitcom and started smiling when she saw Jennifer Aniston eat a bowl of brown rice. "Look, Helen. She's eating brown rice. Pass me some. I'll try it."

Despite her initial protests, she changed her tune and enjoyed the brown rice, which has a nutty flavor. Her famous last words on the subject were: "If it's good enough for Jennifer Aniston, it's good enough for me."

METHOD

Wash the brown rice with cold water and drain. Repeat this process three times until the water runs clear (see tip).

Put the rice in a saucepan or rice cooker and add the cold water. Put the pan over high heat and bring to a boil. Reduce the heat to low, cover with a lid, and simmer for 20 minutes or until all of the liquid has been absorbed.

Remove the pan from the heat and set aside to stand for 5 minutes, still covered with the lid, before serving.

# EGG-FRIED RICE
## 蛋炒飯

Rice has always been viewed as a precious commodity in Guangzhou province, where our grandmother grew up, and it was never wasted. Traditionally, leftover rice is made into egg-fried rice.

The importance of rice to the region is described in this famous folktale. A long, long time ago, five angels riding five rams visited the people of Guangzhou, bringing with them a gift of rice, which was carried in the mouths of the rams, to wish them a bumper harvest. The angels flew away, leaving behind the rams (which turned to stone) to protect the local people from famine.

*Use tamari rather than soy sauce.*

*Dairy free*

*Serves 2*

*Preparation time 5 minutes*

*Cooking time 15 minutes*

**1 tablespoon vegetable oil**

**1 egg, beaten**

**½ cup cooked and cooled long-grain white rice**

**½ teaspoon salt**

**½ teaspoon light soy sauce**

## METHOD
Heat a wok over high heat and add the oil. Add the beaten egg and scramble for 1 minute. Add the rice, reduce the heat to low, and beat out the clumps with a fork to separate the grains. Cook over low heat, tossing and stirring all the time to blend the egg into the rice, until the rice is hot—approx. 5–10 minutes. Sprinkle with the salt, drizzle in some soy sauce, and toss well to combine.

### *Lisa's tips
*The secret to perfect egg-fried rice is to use cooled, boiled rice.*

# VEGETABLE EGG-FRIED RICE
## 雜菜炒飯

This dish was inspired by the delicious paella we enjoyed on a family vacation to Spain. It is a great dish for using up odds and ends of vegetables from the fridge when there aren't enough to make a whole vegetable dish. The crunchy texture of the vegetables makes an interesting change from usual egg-fried rice.

*Use tamari rather than soy sauce.*

*Dairy free*

*Serves 2*

*Preparation time 10 minutes*

*Cooking time 15 minutes*

**2 tablespoons vegetable oil**

**1 egg, beaten**

**½ cup cooled, boiled rice (1 day old is best)**

**1 teaspoon salt**

**1 teaspoon light soy sauce**

**1 carrot, peeled and cut into small dice**

**4 baby corn, cut into small pieces**

**2 asparagus spears, cut into 2-inch pieces**

**1 scallion, finely sliced**

**¾ cup peas**

**1 drop of sesame oil**

## METHOD
Heat a wok over high heat and add 1 tablespoon of oil. Add the beaten egg and scramble for 1 minute, then add the rice. Season with salt and soy sauce and pat out the grains. Cook for 5 minutes. Transfer the rice to a plate and set aside.

Return the wok to the heat and add 1 tablespoon of oil. Stir-fry the vegetables in the hot oil for 5 minutes until cooked through. Return the egg-fried rice to the wok and mix well. Season with a drop of sesame oil and toss through.

# THAI STICKY RICE
# 糯米飯

◑ Use tamari rather than soy sauce.

♥ Dairy free

◐ Egg free

Serves 2

Preparation/soaking time
     3 hours

Cooking time 45 minutes

**½ cup Thai sticky rice**

**6 dried Chinese mushrooms**

**4 large dried shrimps**

**1 dried scallop**

**3 tablespoons vegetable oil**

**1 Chinese sausage (lap cheong),**
   **cut into ½-inch dice**

**½ teaspoon salt**

**1 teaspoon sugar**

**1 scallion, finely sliced**

**\*Lisa's tips**

This is a great alternative to fried rice.

Whenever our mother served this dish, she joked that glutinous rice was the cement that was used to form the Great Wall of China. We found this hilarious. But when I returned to China recently and climbed the Great Wall, I was shocked to see on the front page of the newspaper that chemical tests had proved that parts of the wall's make-up included glutinous sticky rice. I called home to tell my mother the news and she said nonchalantly, "I told you that, and you didn't believe me. Mother's always right!"

This type of rice is called glutinous rice (although it is gluten-free) and when cooked it becomes sticky. This should be distinguished from over-boiled white rice, which turns wet and mushy. Glutinous rice has a distinctive nutty taste and absorbs flavors from other ingredients like a sponge.

## METHOD

Put the rice in a bowl, pour in enough cold water to cover, and set aside to soak for at least 3 hours.

Put the Chinese mushrooms, dried shrimp, and dried scallop in separate bowls and soak in hot water for 15–20 minutes.

Finely chop the mushrooms and shrimp. Shred the scallop into fine shreds, reserving the soaking liquid. Make up to 1 cup using fresh water.

Heat a wok over high heat, add 1 tablespoon of oil, and fry the diced Chinese sausage for 3–4 minutes. Add the shrimp, mushrooms, and scallops and cook for another 3–4 minutes. Set aside.

Tip the soaked rice into a colander and rinse under cold running water to remove excess starch. Drain well.

Heat a wok over high heat and add the remaining oil. Tip in the rice and stir to coat the grains in the oil. Add 2 tablespoons of the reserved soaking liquid and stir over medium heat until all of the liquid has been absorbed.

For best results, try to spread the rice out in a thin layer so it cooks evenly. Continue to add the soaking liquid, 2 tablespoons at a time, until it has all been absorbed. The entire process should take about 25–30 minutes.

Once the rice is cooked, add the salt and sugar and combine well. Stir in the mushroom, sausage and seafood mixture and stir to combine. To serve, spoon the rice into individual bowls and sprinkle with the scallion.

# YANGZHOU FRIED RICE
# 楊州炒飯

🌾 *Use tamari rather than soy sauce.*

♥ *Dairy free*

*Serves 2*

*Preparation time 5 minutes*

*Cooking time 15 minutes*

**2 tablespoons vegetable oil**

**1 egg, beaten**

**½ cup cooled, boiled rice**
  **(1 day old is best)**

**1 teaspoon salt**

**1 teaspoon dark soy sauce**

**1⅓ cups cooked sliced char siu pork**
  *(see page 89)*

**7oz small, cooked, peeled shrimp**

**¾ cup peas**

**1 teaspoon sesame oil**

\*Lisa's tips

*If you don't have any leftover char siu pork,*
*cooked bacon is a great alternative.*

Despite its name, this dish did not originate in Yangzhou. The recipe was invented by Yi Bingshou (1754–1815) during the Qing Dynasty, and the dish was named Yangzhou Fried Rice because Yi was once the regional magistrate of Yangzhou. This popular dish includes char siu, baby shrimp, rice, scallions, and egg and is a good way of using up all the leftovers in the fridge.

METHOD

Heat a wok over high heat and add 1 tablespoon of oil. Add the beaten egg and scramble for 1 minute. Add the rice, season with salt and soy sauce, and pat out the grains to separate them. Cook for 5 minutes, stirring, until the rice has heated through and then tip out onto a plate.

Return the wok to the heat and add the remaining oil. Stir-fry the char siu, shrimp and peas together for 3–5 minutes. Return the egg-fried rice to the pan, add a drop of sesame oil, and mix carefully together to combine.

# HOKKIEN FRIED RICE
## 福建炒飯

*Use tamari rather than soy sauce.*

*Dairy free*

*Serves 2*

*Preparation time 15 minutes*

*Cooking time 20 minutes*

**2 tablespoons vegetable oil**

**1 egg, beaten**

**½ cup cooled, boiled rice
(1 day old is best)**

**pinch of salt**

**1 teaspoon light soy sauce**

*For the topping*

**½ shallot, minced**

**1 garlic clove, minced**

**7oz boneless and skinless chicken
breast, sliced**

**7oz raw, peeled shrimp,
finely chopped**

**3 stems of Chinese broccoli (kai lan)**

**3 Chinese mushrooms, soaked in
boiling water for 15 minutes
then halved**

**1 cup chicken stock** *(see page 12)*

**½ teaspoon salt**

**½ teaspoon sugar**

**1 teaspoon sesame oil**

**1 teaspoon potato starch mixture**
*(see page 8)*

***Lisa's tips**

*This is a perfect dish for using up leftover
meat and vegetables.*

I went to Kuala Lumpur with a family friend when I was younger and the sights and smells made a big impression on me. The air was humid and tropical, laced with the salty tang of the ocean. People were everywhere, rushing back and forth, shouting, smoking, jostling, joking. The scene made my heart race and I clung on tight to Aunty's coat as we disappeared down a street lined with little eateries to find something for lunch. Aunty ordered for me—a plastic bag filled with Coca-Cola, which made my mouth fall open, and a container of Hokkien fried rice. The smell was so fragrant I forgot my manners and tucked into it there and then.

This is my interpretation of the dish I enjoyed that afternoon in Kuala Lumpur. Hokkien fried rice is different from egg-fried rice because of the rich gravy topping, which soaks into the rice infusing it with flavor.

METHOD

Heat a wok over high heat and add 1 tablespoon of oil. Add the beaten egg and scramble for 1 minute before adding the rice. Season with salt and soy sauce, and pat out the grains so the rice warms and separates. Cook for 5 minutes. Remove the rice to a deep bowl and set aside.

Clean the wok, return it to high heat, and add 1 tablespoon of oil. Stir-fry the shallot and garlic briefly to flavor the oil, and then add the chicken, shrimp, Chinese broccoli, and Chinese mushrooms. Stir quickly to coat everything in the flavored oil, pour in the chicken stock, and simmer gently for 5–7 minutes until the chicken is cooked through. Season with the salt, sugar, and sesame oil. Bring to a boil and add the potato starch mixture, stirring vigorously to thicken the sauce.

To serve, pour the chicken and vegetable mixture over the egg-fried rice.

# STEAMED CHICKEN WITH STICKY RICE

*( In a Lotus leaf or Savoy cabbage leaf)*

# 糯米雞

🌾 *Use tamari rather than soy sauce.*

♥ *Dairy free*

◐ *Egg free*

*Serves 2*

*Preparation time 15 minutes (if using cooked sticky rice)*

*Cooking time 40 minutes*

**5oz boneless chicken thighs, finely sliced**

**2 tablespoons vegetable oil**

**4 Chinese mushrooms, soaked in boiling water for 15 minutes and then finely sliced**

**1 Chinese sausage (lap cheong), halved**

**2 large lotus leaves, soaked in lukewarm water for 15 minutes**

**¼ cup cooled, cooked Thai Sticky Rice** *(see page 168)*

**pinch of salt**

**pinch of sugar**

*For the marinade*

**½ teaspoon salt**

**½ teaspoon sugar**

**1 teaspoon dark soy sauce**

**1 teaspoon water**

**1 teaspoon Shaoxing rice wine**

**½ teaspoon sesame oil**

**1 teaspoon potato starch**

**1 teaspoon minced garlic**

**\*Lisa's tips**

*If you can't find lotus leaves use beancurd sheets or even Savoy cabbage leaves.*

Food is often used as an expression of love, and that is certainly true of this dish, where the filling represents love hidden inside a lotus leaf. Love is traditionally repressed in Chinese culture, making the message behind these little parcels even more symbolic. The traditional dish uses dried lotus leaves, which you should be able to find in good Chinese supermarkets. The amazing selection of ingredients that goes into making this flavorful dish makes every bite more meaningful. This recipe uses cooked sticky rice, as shown in the recipe on page 168.

Note that lotus leaves cannot be eaten—they merely hold the filling, infusing it with a subtle tea-leaf flavoring.

METHOD

Combine the chicken in a bowl with all the ingredients for the marinade. Cover the bowl with plastic wrap and transfer to the fridge to marinate for 15 minutes.

Heat a wok over high heat and add the oil. Stir-fry the chicken, mushrooms, and Chinese sausage for 15 minutes or until the chicken is cooked through; set aside.

To assemble the parcels, drain the lotus leaves and put them on a work surface. Divide the cooked rice between the leaves and top with the chicken mixture, allowing half a sausage per leaf. Season with a pinch of salt and sugar. Wrap up the leaves to form a neat package and arrange on a heatproof plate.

To cook the parcels, carefully put the plate inside a preheated steamer and cook for 20 minutes (see page 127).

# XO-STYLE FRIED RICE
# 醬炒飯

*Follow the recipe for XO sauce on page 160, substituting soy sauce for tamari.*

*Dairy free*

*Serves 2*

*Preparation time 5 minutes*

*Cooking time 10 minutes*

**1 tablespoon vegetable oil**

**1 scallion, finely sliced**

**2 eggs, beaten**

**½ cup cooled, boiled rice
(1 day old is best)**

**½ teaspoon salt**

**4 tablespoons XO sauce** *(see page 160)*

**\*Lisa's tips**

*This is a very flavorful recipe for fried rice.
For a deluxe version, add scallops, shrimp
and squid.*

I remember coming back from college one day with a craving for fried rice, but I didn't have many ingredients in the fridge. I did have a jar of XO sauce, however, which was a gift from Dad. So I put the two together and this is what I came up with. The dish was quick to make, it tasted sensational and I devoured it in minutes. In this recipe I have deliberately kept the ingredients for the fried rice to a minimum so that you can really savour the flavor of the sauce, which gets absorbed into every rice grain. If you want to make the XO sauce yourself, follow the recipe on page 160.

METHOD

Heat a wok over high heat and add the oil. Add the scallion and stir briefly to flavor the oil.

Add the beaten egg and scramble it for 1 minute. Add the rice, season with salt and pat out the grains so the rice warms and separates. Cook for 5 minutes, stirring.

Make a well in the center of the rice and add the XO sauce. Stir the sauce into the rice and toss well over high heat before serving.

In many Chinese restaurants, the dessert repertoire is not as wide or varied as in Western counterparts. The tradition after a meal is to eat fresh fruit. For special occasions, such as the Mid-Autumn Moon Festival, Chinese families will eat moon cakes made out of red bean paste with a egg yolk inside. I find them too sweet but our mother loves them. This chapter showcases some more modern and unusual desserts such as the Chile Chocolate Macarons (page 185) and Pear and Ginger Cupcakes (page 186). Toffee Apple or Banana (see page 180) is a universal favorite and even though we're often full after the main meal, there always seems room to squeeze in another piece. For those who aren't craving sugar, we have the fresher options, such as the Mango Pudding (page 182).

Chinese drinks also play a significant part and have a stronger influence than tea. Sweet Mandarin's exotic cocktails will inspire you to create a drink that will get your dinner guests talking and make it a memorable night.

甜點和異國情調的雞尾酒

# DESSERTS & EXOTIC COCKTAILS

# THE BLOODY BARBECUE MARY
## 血腥瑪麗

This is the ultimate hangover cure. We swear by this drink on New Year's Day and you should too. Forget waving the white flag from under the duvet. Drink the Bloody Barbecue Mary and thank the barbecue sauce for casting out your hangover!

- *Gluten free*
- *Dairy free*
- *Egg free*

*Makes 1 x ½ cup cocktail*
*Preparation time 5 minutes*

**¼ cup vodka**
**¼ cup tomato juice**
**2 tablespoons barbecue sauce** *(see page 15)*

METHOD
Pour all the ingredients into a cocktail shaker and add 6 ice cubes. Shake it like crazy. Pour into a tall glass with plenty of ice, and drown your hangover.

**\*Lisa's tips**
*Perfect with a rib of celery and plenty of ice in the glass.*

# THE APHRODISIAC SWEET CHILE STRAWBERRY DAIQUIRI
## 甜辣士多啤梨代基裡酒

Strawberries and chile combined are the ultimate aphrodisiac. You have been warned!

- *Gluten free*
- *Dairy free*
- *Egg free*

*Makes 1 x ¼ cup cocktail*
*Preparation time 5 minutes*

**3 tablespoons white rum**
**1 teaspoon sweet chile sauce** *(see page 14)*
**4 fresh strawberries, plus extra for decorating**
**1½ tablespoons strawberry liqueur**
**sprig of mint, to decorate**

METHOD
Put all the ingredients into a blender along with 6 ice cubes and blend to the consistency of a smoothie. Pour into a glass and decorate with a strawberry and a sprig of mint.

# LONG ISLAND SWEET AND SOUR ICED TEA
## 甜酸長島冰茶

The secret ingredient in this sophisticated dinner drink is Sweet and Sour sauce, which gives the cocktail added smoothness to set it apart from other Long Island Iced Teas. At 22 percent proof, it should help break any awkward silences!

 Gluten free

♥ Dairy free

◐ Egg free

*Makes 1 x 6oz cocktail*

*Preparation time 5 minutes*

2 tablespoons vodka

2 tablespoons tequila

2 tablespoons rum

2 tablespoons gin

2 tablespoons triple sec

2 tablespoons sweet and sour sauce *(see page 14)*

a splash of Coca-Cola

## METHOD
Mix all the ingredients, apart from the Coca-Cola, in a cocktail shaker along with 6 ice cubes. Pour into a tall glass. Add a splash of Coca-Cola and mix with a straw.

## *Lisa's tips
*This has a higher alcohol content than most cocktails due to the small amount of mixer.*

# TOFFEE APPLE OR BANANA
## 拖肥蘋果/香蕉

This is a firm favorite of the family, although we do try to eat it sparingly because of the high sugar content.

◐ Gluten free

♥ Dairy free

*Serves 2*

*Preparation time 10 minutes*

*Cooking time 15 minutes*

2 apples or 2 bananas, peeled

¾ cup cornstarch

1 egg, beaten

²⁄₃ cup plus 1 tablespoon vegetable oil

²⁄₃ cup sugar

1 teaspoon sesame seeds

## METHOD
Slice the apple or banana into 8–10 small pieces and dust lightly with cornstarch. Dip the fruit into the beaten egg and then re-apply the cornstarch.

Preheat ²⁄₃ cup of oil in a wok over high heat to 350°F (see page 35). Carefully lower the fruit into the hot oil and deep-fry for 3 minutes until golden brown. Drain on paper towels and set aside.

Heat 1 tablespoon of oil and sugar in a wok over medium heat, stirring continuously until the sugar has caramelized. Quickly put in the deep-fried fruit pieces and stir gently to coat them in the toffee.

Carefully transfer the caramelized fruit onto a ceramic plate and sprinkle with the sesame seeds. Set aside to cool.

## *Lisa's tips
*To make a slightly healthier version, leave out the caramel step and drizzle some maple syrup over the top instead.*

# FRESH MANGO PAVLOVA
## 芒果奶油蛋白餅

*Gluten free*

*Dairy free*

*Serves 2*

*Preparation time 20 minutes*

*Cooking time 1 hour*

**4 egg whites**

**1 cup sugar**

**1 teaspoon vanilla extract**

**1 teaspoon lemon juice**

**1 teaspoon cornstarch**

**⅓ cup fresh mango, cut into 1-inch dice**

**¼ cup mango juice or nectar**

**\*Lisa's tips**

*Mango is great with meringue. You could also add some passionfruit seeds if you wish.*

When we were small, our mother often used to make us a pavlova as our birthday cake, saying she'd stolen a piece of the clouds and whipped up a little piece of Heaven just for us. We were ecstatic and loved crunching the crispy peaks—we were so impressed she could climb so high to reach the clouds! Mangoes were also popular in our house, so much so that Mom and Dad used to buy them in boxes of six!

METHOD

Preheat the oven to 250°F and line a baking sheet with parchment paper.

Whisk the egg whites with an electric mixer until they have doubled in volume. Gradually add the sugar, vanilla extract, lemon juice, and cornstarch and continue to whisk on full speed until the egg whites form stiff peaks, approx. 10 minutes.

Spoon the meringue mixture onto the prepared baking sheet to form 10 meringues, each approx. 2 inches in diameter.

Bake the meringues in the preheated oven for 1 hour or until they sound crisp and hollow when tapped underneath. Remove from the oven and set aside to cool.

To make the mango compote, put the diced mango and mango juice in a saucepan and bring to a boil. Boil rapidly for 2–3 minutes until the sauce thickens, and then remove from the heat and set aside to cool.

To serve, arrange the pavlovas on a plate and spoon on the mango sauce.

# MANGO PUDDING
# 芒果布丁

Gluten free

Egg free

*Serves 2*

*Preparation time 15 minutes*

*Setting time up to 2 hours*

**2 teaspoons of gelatin**

**½ cup hot water**

**1 large fresh mango**

**⅔ cup canned mango slices,**
   **blended in a food processor**

**½ cup evaporated milk**

**10 ice cubes**

**5 tablespoons sugar**

**2 sprigs of mint, to decorate**

### *Lisa's tips

*Make in advance and serve as a delicious
refreshing dessert.*

Mango Pudding is probably the most popular Chinese dessert. This is delicious served cold and perfect to prepare in advance for a party.

METHOD

Put the gelatin in a small bowl, pour in the hot water, and set aside until the gelatin dissolves, approx. 2 minutes.

Meanwhile, cut the fresh mango in half and dice the flesh of one half. Set aside the other half to use for decoration.

In a large bowl, mix together the blended canned mango slices, evaporated milk, and ice cubes. Pour the gelatin mixture into the mango mixture and mix well with a spoon until the ice cubes have melted. Add the fresh diced mango, stir in the sugar, and pour into two molds, 4 inches in diameter. Transfer to the fridge to set for 1½–2 hours.

To serve, turn out the puddings onto a serving plate, decorate with a few slices of fresh mango, and garnish with sprigs of mint.

# CHILE CHOCOLATE MACARONS
# 辣朱古力夾心餅

*Gluten free*

*Makes 10*

*Preparation time 45 minutes*

*Cooking time 15 minutes*

**1 cup almond flour**

**1¼ cups confectioner's sugar**

**pinch of cayenne pepper**

**3 egg whites**

**½ teaspoon cream of tartar**

**2 tablespoons sugar**

*For the chile chocolate filling*

**5oz dark chocolate (approx. 70 percent cocoa solids), chopped**

**⅔ cup heavy cream**

**pinch of cayenne pepper**

**1 tablespoon unsalted butter**

**\*Lisa's tips**

*Don't be put off by the cayenne— it's very subtle and goes really well with the chocolate.*

I remember being fascinated by the macaron tower challenge on *Masterchef* and wondering what this delightful tower tasted like. "It's pronounced 'mack-her-on,' not 'macaroon'," the presenter crooned. "We're not talking coconut macaroons; we're talking French delicatessens." Wow, I thought. That is one challenge I would love to face one day. I parked that thought until I appeared at a farmers' market to sell our gluten-free sauces, where I was stationed next to a baker named Louise selling macarons. We had a good laugh and in exchange for three bottles of our Sweet Mandarin sauces, I received a selection of macarons in all different flavors. There and then I fell in love with these bite-sized delicacies—which are far superior to any cookie I have ever tasted. Typical flavors are chocolate, strawberry, pistachio, lemon, and raspberry. However, I love experimenting with my own flavors and came up with this combination.

METHOD

Mix the almond flour, confectioner's sugar, and cayenne pepper together in a food processor and set aside.

In a separate bowl, whisk together the egg whites, cream of tartar, and sugar until stiff peaks form. Carefully fold the almond mixture into the egg white mixture until thoroughly combined.

Spoon the macaron mixture into a piping bag fitted with a ½-inch round nozzle and pipe twenty 1-inch circles onto a baking sheet lined with parchment paper. Set aside to rest on the baking sheet for 20 minutes or until a skin forms.

Meanwhile, preheat the oven to 325°F and prepare the chocolate filling. Melt the chocolate in a heatproof bowl over a saucepan of barely simmering water. Remove the bowl from the heat and beat in the cream, cayenne pepper, and unsalted butter. Set aside to cool.

Bake the macarons in the preheated oven for 15 minutes until puffed up and golden. Remove them from the oven and set aside to cool on the baking sheet for 5 minutes before transferring them to a wire rack to cool completely.

To assemble the macarons, sandwich two cooled macarons together with 1 tablespoon of the cooled chocolate cream.

# PEAR AND GINGER CUPCAKES
鳳梨蛋糕

*Use gluten-free flour instead of self-rising.*

*Makes approx. 24*

*Preparation time 15 minutes*

*Cooking time 15 minutes*

8 tablespoons (1 stick) softened
    butter

½ cup sugar

2 eggs, beaten

¾ cup self-rising flour

1 teaspoon ground cinnamon

½ teaspoon nutmeg

pinch of salt

2 tablespoons low-fat milk

2 Asian pears, peeled, cored. and
    chopped into small cubes

1 tablespoon candied ginger, cut into
    small pieces

confectioner's sugar, for dusting

\*Lisa's tips

*You can substitute almonds for the candied ginger if you wish.*

These days, you can't go anywhere without seeing cupcakes. When I was young, we used to call them fairy cakes—and that is exactly what they were, little cakes that you could finish in three bites. Today cupcakes are literally the size of a cup, and I find them much too much—and they're not helpful for the waistline either!

For this recipe, I have kept to the old-fashioned size, which cooks more quickly, resulting in a moister cake. The yin (ginger) and yang (Chinese pear) flavorings complement each other beautifully.

METHOD

Line two 12-hole muffin pans with paper cases. Preheat the oven to 400°F.

Cream the butter and sugar together in a bowl until light and creamy. Gradually beat in the eggs, a little at a time, and then fold in the flour, ground cinnamon, nutmeg, and salt. Mix to a dropping consistency with the milk. Finally add the pears and candied ginger and combine thoroughly.

Carefully spoon the mixture into the paper cases and bake in the oven for 15 minutes until golden and springy to the touch.

Remove from the oven and transfer to a wire rack to cool. Dust with confectioner's sugar to serve and top with a small piece of ginger if you wish.

# FORTUNE COOKIES
## 幸運曲奇餅

*Use gluten-free flour.*

*Dairy free*

*Makes 12*

*Preparation time 15 minutes*

*Cooking time 20 minutes*

**1¼ cups all-purpose flour**

**¼ cup cornstarch**

**3 tablespoons sugar**

**¼ cup water**

**¼ cup vegetable oil**

**2 egg whites**

**1 teaspoon vanilla extract**

**pinch of salt**

**\*Lisa's tips**

*These are perfect for a party. Write your own messages to pass on your good wishes to your guests.*

Fortune cookies do not actually originate from China but from America. However, they are great fun and many people associate them with Chinese restaurants. The non-Chinese origin of the fortune cookie is humorously illustrated in Amy Tan's 1989 novel *The Joy Luck Club*, in which a pair of immigrant women from China find jobs at a fortune cookie factory in America. They are amused by the unfamiliar concept of a fortune cookie but, after several hilarious attempts at translating the fortunes into Chinese, come to the conclusion that the cookies contain not wisdom but "bad instruction."

METHOD

Write your fortune messages on small rectangles of white paper, about 1 x ½ inch.

Mix all the ingredients together in a bowl.

Heat a large frying pan over high heat. Drop in 1 tablespoon of the batter and cook for 5 minutes until set. Flip over the cookie and cook for 1 minute on the other side.

Remove the cookie from the heat with a spatula and transfer it to a plate. Put the message on top and fold the cookie in half to form a semicircle, pressing the edges together to seal. To create the curved shape, hold the cookie at each end and press the folded edge against a cup. Transfer the fortune cookie to an empty egg carton to cool and settle into shape while you make the rest.

The fortune cookies are ready to serve once they have hardened, after approx. 10 minutes. If you don't want to eat them immediately, they can be stored in an airtight container for up to a week.